• DOG BREED HANDBOOKS •

LABRADOR
RETRIEVER

• DOG BREED HANDBOOKS •

LABRADOR RETRIEVER

DR. BRUCE FOGLE

SPECIAL PHOTOGRAPHY BY
TRACY MORGAN

DORLING KINDERSLEY
LONDON · NEW YORK · STUTTGART · MOSCOW

A DORLING KINDERSLEY BOOK

Project Editor JILL FORNARY
Art Editor SARAH GOODWIN
Editor SARAH LILLICRAPP
Designer WENDY BARTLET
Managing Editor FRANCIS RITTER
Managing Art Editor DEREK COOMBES
DTP Designer CRESSIDA JOYCE
Picture Researcher JO CARLILL
Production Controller ADRIAN GATHERCOLE

First published in Great Britain in 1996
by Dorling Kindersley Limited,
9 Henrietta Street, London WC2E 8PS

A CIP catalogue record for this book is
available from the British Library

ISBN 0 7513 0267 8

Reproduced by Colourscan, Singapore
Printed and bound in Italy by Graphicom

CONTENTS

INTRODUCTION

Many centuries of evolution have produced today's domestic dog breeds from their common wolf ancestor. Over 15,000 years ago, when our ancient relatives first created semi-permanent settlements, local wolves in turn moved into the areas surrounding the encampments to scavenge for food. Only the smallest and tamest of these "self-domesticated" wolves survived, and within a very short time the modified wolf-dog had emerged. The early human settlers, recognizing potential uses for these creatures, began capturing young cubs and raising them to protect their campsites and assist in hunting.

It seems difficult to believe that the wolf is a relative, no matter how distant, of the lovable Labrador

This 19th-century aristocrat's companion was selectively bred to retrieve game on hunts

ADAPTATION OF THE BREED

By about 6,000 years ago, selective breeding by humans had produced many different dog breeds with enhanced qualities for specific roles, including guarding, load-bearing, herding, and hunting. More recently, only in the last 1,000 years, people have amassed sufficient wealth to hunt purely for pleasure, leading to the development of the sporting dog. The Labrador Retriever is a supreme example of this most advanced branch of canines, for it performs in an unnatural way – adeptly finding wounded prey but rather than instinctively eating it, carefully bringing the game back to its waiting master.

The Labrador happily retrieves from all terrains; its ancestors used to drag in fishing nets from the icy waters of Newfoundland

Despite their inherently friendly nature, Labradors can be loyal protectors of the home, barking to defend their territory

NATURAL PROTECTIVE INSTINCTS

The Labrador's specific development, first to assist fishermen and later as a gundog, has enhanced its eagerness to serve its owner and work co-operatively with other dogs. Yet even this most gentle, sweet-tempered breed has not lost its innate canine instincts, which may be expressed though natural guarding or defence.

THE IDEAL COMPANION

The modern Labrador Retriever was developed expressly as a sporting breed – to work to the gun, retrieving game for huntsmen. Its exceptional abilities have, however, led to a variety of other roles. Labradors are among the finest scent-detecting dogs, and are widely used in all types of rescue work, and in the detection of drugs and explosives.

Excellent gundogs and always happy to work as a team, Labradors are highly adept at scenting and retrieving game

The Labrador's affable character and superb responsiveness to training have also made it an exemplary assistant for the disabled – in fact, it is the world's most successful guide dog for the blind. But for many devotees of the breed, the Labrador Retriever's most outstanding characteristic is its happy, affectionate nature and overwhelming dedication to its owner. It is a perfect companion for both adults and children, and its well-deserved international popularity continues to grow with each passing year.

The Labrador's retrieving skills are second to none – any type of game is held with a "soft mouth" and willingly surrendered on command

THE IDEAL CHOICE

THE AMIABLE LABRADOR RETRIEVER'S reputation as a family dog is
fully justified, but owners of this affectionate and energetic
breed must be prepared to cope with their Labrador's lively,
sometimes over-exuberant nature, as well as accommodate its
great need for outdoor activity and vigorous exercise.

INTEGRAL PART OF THE FAMILY

*Labrador is
happiest when
taking part
in family life*

*Children and
dog enjoy
each other's
company*

A dog can provide great
companionship and
affection, but you
must be prepared to
care for your pet for
at least the next 13
years. Like a child, it
depends on you for
its health and well-
being. Consider not
only the cost of
food and veterinary
attention, but also
the time you must
commit as an owner.

A HAPPY AND BOISTEROUS BREED

A BOUNDING "HELLO"
It is possible to be literally
bowled over by a typical
welcome from an
enthusiastic Labrador.
This warm, friendly
nature is part of the
breed's appeal, but
your dog's eager spirit
and very tactile zest
for life can actually
be a dangerous
nuisance if
uncontrolled.

TAIL-WAGGING MAYHEM
In their exuberance, Labradors tend to be a
little clumsy. This may at first be endearing,
but can quickly become exasperating. The
Labrador's thick, muscular tail is at a perfect
height to sweep low table surfaces clean.
Contemplate a vivacious Labrador only if
you are prepared for occasional accidents!

*Dog leaps up
excitedly to greet
new friend*

BOUNDING WITH ENERGY

Although a popular pet, Labradors were originally bred to work outdoors, and thrive on physical and mental activity. Consider acquiring this energetic and responsive breed only if you can provide it with the space, exercise, and attention it needs.

PREPARE FOR HAIR!

Although its coat is relatively short, the Labrador's hair is quite harsh, and when shed has a tendency to stick into materials. This can make it quite difficult to remove from clothing, upholstery, and carpets. Therefore, a Labrador is perhaps not the perfect type of dog for the exceptionally house-proud. Dogs that live outdoors in kennels moult twice yearly, but those kept in centrally heated environments often shed hair all year round. If you still want a Labrador, it is worth considering the colour of your home furnishings and even your favourite clothes before finally deciding whether a yellow, chocolate, or black dog is best for you.

AN AFFABLE, OBEDIENT COMPANION

With its willing, sociable character and even disposition, the Labrador has all the makings of an ideal dog. Yet these qualities must be nurtured, and it is only through dedicated training that even the most sweet-natured dog becomes a truly rewarding companion. From the moment you become an owner, you will need to invest time, introducing your Labrador to new situations and always teaching good conduct. A well-mannered dog is a pleasure both for you and others.

Well-trained Labrador interacts happily with strangers and other animals

BREED CHARACTERISTICS

THE LABRADOR RETRIEVER'S OFFICIAL breed standard was originally developed by people who used this obedient, happy dog as a working companion. Today, the standard continues to emphasize the gentle, eager-to-please nature of this most affable of dogs, as well as a body conformation eminently suited for working on land and in water.

MUSCULAR AND WELL BALANCED
The Labrador stands firmly on solid, powerful forelimbs. Its toes are webbed for speed and endurance when swimming, while the chest is not excessively wide, allowing easy movement of the well-muscled legs.

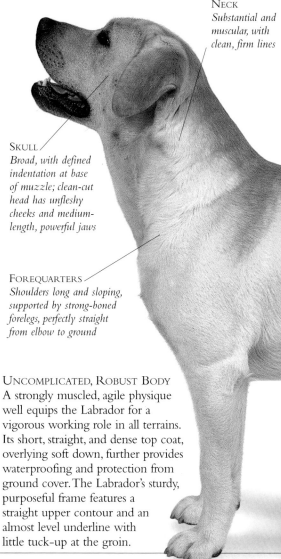

NECK
Substantial and muscular, with clean, firm lines

SKULL
Broad, with defined indentation at base of muzzle; clean-cut head has unfleshy cheeks and medium-length, powerful jaws

FOREQUARTERS
Shoulders long and sloping, supported by strong-boned forelegs, perfectly straight from elbow to ground

UNCOMPLICATED, ROBUST BODY
A strongly muscled, agile physique well equips the Labrador for a vigorous working role in all terrains. Its short, straight, and dense top coat, overlying soft down, further provides waterproofing and protection from ground cover. The Labrador's sturdy, purposeful frame features a straight upper contour and an almost level underline with little tuck-up at the groin.

GOOD-NATURED, DEVOTED COMPANION
With a typically wide head and slightly
pronounced brows, even this distinctively
masculine Labrador has a gentle look
which is synonymous with the breed.

EYES
*Friendly, medium-
sized dark eyes are
placed well apart*

EARS
*Close-hanging,
neither large nor
heavy, and
set rather
far back*

NOSE
*Wide nose
with large
nostrils on
broad muzzle*

TEETH
*Upper teeth closely
overlap lower in
"scissors" bite*

DIVERGING BREED STANDARDS

Differences in height and overall
shape between working or field-trial
Labradors and show Labradors are
becoming so great that separate
standards may eventually be
established. Modifications to the
standard in the United States specify
considerably taller, lankier dogs than
original English requirements, and
this may lead to the development of
a distinctive American variety, as has
already occurred with the Cocker
Spaniel. Nevertheless, any breed
standard for the Labrador will always
prize a biddable, easy-going character
as highly as practical working ability.

DOUBLE COAT
*Short, dense outer coat without
feathering or waving covers soft,
waterproof down*

BACK
*Top line of body is level,
carried above short, wide,
and strong loins*

TAIL
*Medium-length,
rounded, "otter-
like" tail is very
thick at base,
gradually tapering
to tip, with no
feathering*

HINDQUARTERS
*Broad, muscular, and
very strongly developed,
straight and not sloping
to tail, with sturdy, well-
defined thighs*

BODY
*Chest well muscled and
powerfully built, of good
width and depth, with
barrel-shaped ribcage*

FEET
*Rounded and compact,
with well-arched, webbed
toes and generous pads*

MEASUREMENTS (BRITISH BREED STANDARD)
Height at withers (see page 77):
FEMALE 54–56 cm (21.5–22 in)
MALE 56–57 cm (22–22.5 in)
Weight, in proportion to height:
FEMALE 25–32 kg (55–70 lb)
MALE 27–36 kg (60–80 lb)

1.5 m
(6 ft)

BEHAVIOUR PROFILE

EVERY DOG HAS ITS OWN personality, moulded in part by its experiences within the litter, and later with you. Heredity is the other important factor, bringing both positive and negative traits for each breed. Overall, the Labrador Retriever's willing, genial disposition has made it an enduring favourite.

TRAINABILITY/OBEDIENCE

Labrador Retrievers are considered the most trainable of all breeds, followed closely by German Shepherds, Australian Cattle Dogs, and Golden Retrievers. Originally bred specifically to work under human direction, they have a co-operative spirit and are very responsive to instruction, typically showing great loyalty and obedience to their owners.

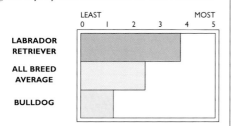

PLAYFULNESS WITH OTHER DOGS

The Labrador scores as the most playful of all breeds, surpassing the Golden Retriever, English Springer Spaniel, and Irish Setter – all gundogs also bred to work in the field with other dogs. Labradors are naturally gregarious, fun-loving, and inquisitive, and will normally seize any opportunity for friendly interaction with other canines.

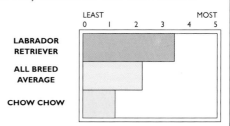

BARKING TO PROTECT THE HOME

Other than the Newfoundland, there is no breed rated poorer at barking to defend its home than the Labrador Retriever. The friendly Labrador is more likely to show burglars around! However, it may well bowl over intruders with a bounding welcome.

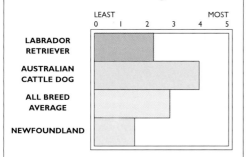

NEED FOR PHYSICAL ACTIVITY

Coming from a working background, the energetic Labrador thrives on physical and mental activity. Only the Australian Kelpie and Cattle Dog and the Chesapeake Bay Retriever have a greater need, although early experience influences this trait even more than heredity.

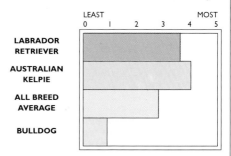

How to Use the Behaviour Charts

In a recent study, vets and dog breeders have assessed over 100 breeds, rating each on a scale of 0–5 for specific personality traits, with 0 representing the lowest score among all dogs and 5 the highest. Here, for eight different behaviours, the Labrador Retriever is compared with the statistically "average" canine, as well as the breeds reported at both extremes for each characteristic. These findings do not take into consideration either sex or coat colour.

Reliable with Strange Children

The even-tempered, amiable Labrador is among the most dependable of all breeds when meeting unfamiliar children. Even so, an adult should always be present, and children, until emotionally mature, should never be left alone even with the gentlest of dogs.

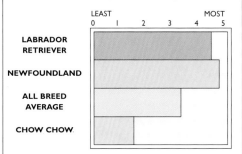

Calm in New Circumstances

Labradors, in common with Newfoundlands, Golden Retrievers, Cairn Terriers, and French Bulldogs, tend to be unperturbed by strange sounds, surroundings, or people. This reflects the breed's development as a gundog and adaptable, easy-going, curious nature.

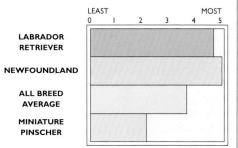

Non-destructive when Alone

Labradors are only slightly more likely than the "average" dog to be destructive when left unattended. Scratching on walls, digging in carpets or gardens, or chewing furniture is less common in well-exercised dogs, given mentally stimulating toys to avert boredom.

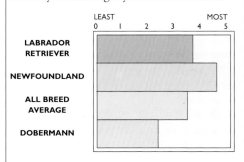

House Trainable

Virtually all dogs respond fairly well to house training, but the Labrador Retriever and the German Shepherd are regarded as the most receptive. Both breeds have a great aptitude for learning, general eagerness to please, and exceptionally willing, dutiful characters.

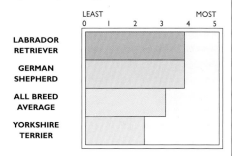

COATS AND COLOURS

LABRADORS COME IN THREE "VARIETIES": yellow, black, and chocolate. Eyes are usually a warm hazel or brown with dark rims, and the nose black or dark brown, although a yellow dog's nose may fade to pink in winter. The coat is dense and waterproof, and curiously its colour can have some bearing on personality.

YELLOW AND BLACK COATS

Matings between yellow Labradors always produce yellow offspring. Black Labradors, however, may bear either all black puppies or a mixed litter. Professional breeders usually know whether their black stock carries the potential to produce yellow. Vets and breeders generally find no differences between yellows and blacks in characteristics such as trainability, playfulness with other dogs, or enjoyment at being petted. However, yellow Labradors are considered slightly more likely to whine for attention, and to bark when anxious or to protect the home. They may also be moderately more excitable, and more destructive when left alone, although all these behaviour variations are very minor.

DOUBLE TROUBLE
Both colours can appear in one litter.

VARIATIONS OF YELLOW
Colour intensity ranges from champagne cream, through rich golden, to the more unusual fox-red.

GLOSSY BLACK
This black Labrador has a typically strong yet gentle face with noble features.

CHOCOLATE LABRADORS

This rich, attractive coat colour is relatively rare, but becoming increasingly popular. Both yellow and black Labradors may produce chocolate-coloured puppies, but the genetics are complicated. In theory, all three colours can appear in one litter – and occasionally this does happen. However, when matters are left to nature alone, just one puppy in eight is born with chocolate pigmentation. Breeders normally prefer to avoid using yellow stock to produce chocolate offspring, as these puppies sometimes have very pale skin and light eyes.

DEEP BROWN
Shades vary from a liver colour to rich, dark brown.

MATURE FEMALE
This bitch gave birth to all chocolate puppies, including the dog above.

NATURAL-BORN SWIMMERS

A BREED THAT REVELS IN GETTING WET
If water is available – from the smallest of puddles to a vast ocean, no matter how dirty or salty – Labradors will find it, and dive in with relish. The breed's powerful, muscular legs, well-proportioned chest, and webbed toes are perfectly designed for speed and endurance when swimming.

DENSE, WATERPROOF UNDERCOAT
The Labrador Retriever has inherited a thick, woolly undercoat from its Canadian ancestors, bred for work in the cold waters of Newfoundland. This specially-adapted layer gives superb, waterproof insulation, although Labradors can still suffer from hypothermia in severe conditions.

SEX AND TYPE DIFFERENCES

APART FROM THEIR OBVIOUS physical differences, male and female Labradors can also vary somewhat in character. Specific "types" bred primarily for working or showing may differ too. Yet all have in common the willing nature and eminent trainability that distinguish this justly popular breed.

PHYSIQUE AND TEMPERAMENT: THE SEXES COMPARED

Male Labradors are typically larger and more powerfully built than females, and have less delicate features. In behaviour, gender-related differences are very minor, with males only slightly more dominant. Overall, both sexes are very even-tempered and highly trainable.

GENTLE, RESPONSIVE FEMALE
Female Labradors are often considered marginally easier to train than males, and less likely to disobey their owners. They also tend to be more playful with other dogs. Neutering usually has little effect on a bitch's personality, but can sometimes reduce an inclination towards possessiveness.

Head is narrower and body is slighter than male's

GENDER-SPECIFIC MEDICAL PROBLEMS

A variety of diseases are caused or influenced by sex hormones. Unless spayed early in life, females of all breeds may suffer from breast cancer and pyometra, or womb infection. Uncastrated males sometimes develop perianal tumours, testicular cancer, or prostate disorders, with associated pain or bleeding on urination. Neutering is part of the preferred treatment for all gender-related medical conditions, but in Labradors particularly, neutering must be followed by careful diet control to prevent weight gain.

CONFIDENT MALE
Males tend to have a more wilful nature than females, and therefore can be slightly more headstrong and disobedient. However, unlike numerous other breeds, male Labradors are not markedly more aggressive than females. Although they may be instinctively assertive with other male dogs, dominance is more likely to take the form of rowdiness rather than belligerence.

Male has larger, heavier body and broader head

SHOW OR WORKING TYPE?

"PERFECT" LOOKS
Many Labradors are bred primarily to conform to formal show standards. The notion of an ideal specimen continues to vary somewhat over time and from country to country, since the official breed standard may be interpreted fluidly. For many years, Labradors in the USA were bred to be considerably larger than the favoured European size. Now these preferences have been more clearly defined in a new American standard. Whichever standard is used, dogs intended for exhibition are first bred for beauty and then trained from an early age in show-ring deportment.

Wide, solidly structured head with slightly pronounced eyebrows

Stocky, muscular build with well-developed chest and powerful hindquarters

Long, sloping shoulders supported by straight, sturdily-boned forelegs

Working Labrador's physique is slimmer and lighter-framed, for nimble activity in the field

BRED TO WORK
Although all Labradors can be trained as gundogs or for working trials, requiring skills in obedience, agility, or scent trailing, some are bred specifically for such roles. They may still meet show standards, but often have lighter, leaner bodies which are considered more agile in the field. Working dogs are also bred to have an exceptionally strong retrieving instinct and a keen responsiveness to training.

SELECTIVE BREEDING FOR SPECIAL ROLES

Labradors and Golden Retrievers are the world's most successful assistance dogs, trained to help people with disabilities. Just as dogs destined for other roles are selectively bred to enhance certain desirable qualities, in recent years dogs have been bred specifically for assistance work, with the most important criteria being sound health and a calm, unflappable disposition.

Guide dog bred not for show quality, but for working ability

FINDING THE RIGHT DOG

HAVING DECIDED THAT you want to acquire a Labrador, be selective in your search. Do not act impulsively; seek professional guidance from your local vet or dog training club, and choose carefully according to this advice and your lifestyle. Any purchase should incorporate a veterinary examination.

ADVICE ON WHERE TO BUY AND WHAT TO LOOK FOR

CONSULT A VETERINARIAN

Vets and their staff can provide unbiased information on what to look for in a healthy Labrador Retriever. They are usually aware of any prevalent medical problems or behavioural idiosyncracies, and their advice is always free of charge.

INQUIRE AT LOCAL DOG TRAINING CLUBS

Contact a local dog club for guidance on how to find a trainable Labrador. Trainers can often also recommend breeders who produce dogs specifically for field work or showing. While gender and coat colour partly determine a dog's temperament, so do breeding lines.

SUITABLE FOR YOUR LIFESTYLE?

Select a dog that fits into your daily routine both now and as you foresee it in years to come. Labradors are large, energetic dogs, needing lots of exercise and mental stimulation. If you are new to the breed, talk to other owners about their dogs and try to spend some time with one. If you have a family, all decisions on buying a dog should be made together.

Pet Labrador Retriever is established as well-loved member of family

Deciding on a Puppy or an Adult Dog

Buying a Pure-bred Puppy

Although puppies are undoubtedly appealing, they are also extremely lively and demand plenty of attention; be prepared! Reputable breeders are the best source for Labrador puppies. Visit several litters before making your choice, and note the physique and temperament of the mother and, if possible, the father too. Resist the temptation to buy the first puppy that takes your fancy.

Animal Rescue Centres

Animal shelters always have dogs needing good homes. A rescued Labrador is more likely to have behaviour problems, notably destructive activity when left alone. Yet, "recycled" dogs can settle in and make loyal, affectionate companions. An adult rescued dog may be a good option if you want to avoid the bother of house training a puppy, and are willing to cope with any unexpected personality quirks.

Health Checks for Your New Dog

Vet gives puppy thorough health examination

Make any purchase conditional upon your vet's confirmation that the dog is healthy, with no sign of infectious disease, malnutrition, or parasites. Breeders should provide documents verifying that a puppy's parents are free from a variety of hereditary disorders. By law, if a puppy is not healthy at purchase, you are entitled to a refund or a replacement. It is wise to place a similar condition on the purchase of an adult dog regardless of the source.

Avoid Puppy Mills

Whenever possible, buy your dog directly from a reputable breeder, either professional or amateur. Avoid puppy farms or mills, as they often provide inhumane environments for mothers and give little attention to the puppies' health. Newspaper advertisements can sometimes be fronts for mills; be suspicious if when visiting a private home you cannot see the litter's mother. Be wary also of pet shops; they can be fertile environments for a variety of infectious diseases, and may supply you with an unhealthy specimen purchased from a puppy mill.

YOUR NEW PUPPY

IDEALLY, BUY YOUR LABRADOR puppy from a recommended breeder when it is about eight weeks old. Older puppies may find it harder adapting to a new home. Make a careful choice after viewing several litters, then get everything ready to help ensure a smooth introduction for all.

CHOOSING THE RIGHT PUPPY

VISITING A LITTER
Watch the puppies together; some may be retiring, others more bold. Remember that the most outgoing puppy may grow up to be the most independent adult, while the most withdrawn could become the shyest. Decide which sex you prefer, then select a puppy that seems bright, alert, and healthy.

Confident puppy enjoys being handled

Puppy is relaxed and content

THE ONE FOR YOU?
When picking up or holding a very young puppy, always support its hindquarters. The puppy should feel firm, and surprisingly heavy. Ask to see the parents' registration documents, and certificates verifying that they are free from hereditary medical conditions, including eye diseases and hip dysplasia. Ultimately, of course, your final decision will rest on a particular puppy's looks and unique, endearing behaviour.

MEET THE PARENTS

Responsible breeders are proud of their breeding stock and will be delighted to introduce you to the litter's mother and also the father if available. The parents' appearance and behaviour will give some idea of your puppy's mature size and likely temperament. Do not buy a puppy from individuals who are unable to show you the mother; they may not be genuine breeders but agents for puppy mills. All reputable breeders will also permit you to return a puppy immediately if your vet feels there is good reason to do so.

Settling in at Home

Getting Acquainted

As soon as you arrive home with your new puppy, introduce it to its own "den" – a crate lined with soft bedding is ideal. Initially, make the crate inviting by placing food treats or toys inside, and leave the door open. When the door is shut, a resident dog can investigate without fear of harassment.

First Night Alone

The first night that your puppy is away from its brothers and sisters and in new surroundings is always the most difficult. Provide it with a chewable toy for comfort and, if you are willing, place the crate in your bedroom so the puppy is reassured by your presence. Do not respond to plaintive cries, however, or you will unwittingly train your puppy to whine for attention.

Puppy is distressed and tries to climb out of crate

Sweet Dreams

With a little perseverance, your puppy will learn to settle down and sleep. Set your alarm so that you can get up during the night for the first few weeks to take your puppy to relieve itself. Alternatively, line one side of the crate with bedding and the other with newspaper for soiling. When your puppy is a bit older, it should happily accept sleeping outside of your bedroom.

EARLY TRAINING

AS SOON AS YOU BRING your puppy home, begin gentle training for obedience and hygiene. Reward good behaviour with praise, stroking, or food treats. Provide toys to keep your puppy alert and occupied, and arrange regular contact with other dogs to ensure proper social development.

LEARNING WITH REWARDS

VERBAL PRAISE

Labradors are eager pupils and learn quickly. Even a very young puppy will be sensitive to your manner and tone of voice, and will understand when you are genuinely pleased with its behaviour. Enthusiastic words of approval should always accompany any other type of reward.

Touching the head can be threatening; stroke puppy on its body instead

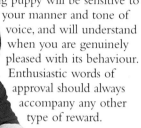

Puppy knows it has done well when it hears "Good dog!"

STROKING REWARD

Touch is an intensely powerful reward. Your puppy will naturally want to be stroked, but do not comply on demand. Offer petting in response to good conduct, so that obedience is associated with desired physical attention.

ACQUIRING SOCIAL SKILLS

A puppy's ability to learn is at its greatest during the first three months. If denied ongoing contact with other dogs during this important stage, your Labrador Retriever may not develop the social skills necessary for meeting strange dogs later in life. If you do not have another dog, ask your vet to help you organize weekly "puppy parties" to encourage natural, friendly interaction with other healthy puppies.

Edible rewards work well with most Labradors

FOOD TREAT

The Labrador gives the impression that a large portion of its brain is dedicated to a constant search for food. Exploit this breed characteristic by using low–calorie treats such as vitamin tablets as primary rewards, reinforced with vigorous praise.

TOYS FOR YOUR NEW PUPPY

Chew toy with plaited rope exercises puppy's jaw muscles

SUITABLE TOYS FOR CHEWING AND PLAYING
Good toys are designed to stimulate your puppy both physically and mentally. Dogs are particularly attracted to toys with distinctive odours, and ones that are fun to chase, capture, retrieve, or chew. Take special care with squeaky toys; curious Labradors are prone to accidentally swallowing the "squeakers".

TOYS AS REWARD AND COMFORT
While toys left lying around soon become boring, items brought out only under special circumstances are transformed into exciting rewards. Give toys selectively as a prize for good behaviour, and put them away after use so your dog understands that they belong to you. Whenever you leave your Labrador alone, provide a favourite toy as soothing distraction.

HOUSE TRAINING INDOORS AND OUT

PAPER TRAINING
Your puppy will usually want to eliminate after waking, eating, drinking, or exercise. It may signal this by putting its nose down and sniffing. Quickly place the dog in an area covered with newspaper, and praise it when it urinates or messes. It is pointless to punish your puppy after an accident. If you catch it in the act, however, say "No" in a stern tone to teach it that it must use the paper.

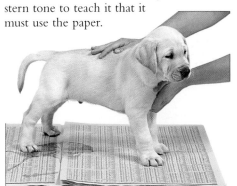

MOVING OUTSIDE
Start outdoor training as soon as possible. Three-month-old Labrador puppies need to empty their bladders about every three hours. Take a small piece of soiled paper with you; the puppy will smell its own scent, and be encouraged to transfer toileting outside. As it eliminates, say "Hurry up"; this will train your dog to relieve itself on that command.

INTRODUCING OUTDOORS

ALL PUPPIES SHOULD EXPERIENCE the outdoors as soon as possible. Provide essential vaccinations and identification, and accustom your young Labrador to a collar and lead. Ask friends to help you create situations in which the puppy can meet new people and other dogs in controlled circumstances.

IDENTIFICATION

STANDARD NAME TAG
Engraved or canister tags carry vital information about your dog, including a contact telephone number. When possible, also list your vet's emergency telephone number. A touch of nail varnish will prevent metal canisters from unscrewing.

Registration number is stored in this tiny microchip

PERMANENT METHODS
Painless tattoos on the ear, bearing a number registered with a kennel club or other private organization, provide permanent identification, and are widely popular. More recently, microchips have also been introduced. Inserted just under the skin on the neck, they are "read" using a hand-held scanner.

INTRODUCTION TO COLLAR AND LEAD

1 Collar and lead training can begin as soon as you acquire your puppy. Start by letting the dog see and smell the collar. Then, avoiding eye contact, kneel down and put the collar on, distracting with words. Reward your puppy with treats, physical contact, and praise. Actively play for a while, then take the collar off. Your puppy will quickly learn to associate the collar with rewards, and should accept it without reluctance.

Put on a light, comfortable collar, distracting puppy with words, or using a treat or toy

Reward puppy for accepting lead by giving access to toy

2 Once your puppy is content wearing its collar, kneel in front and attach a lead. Keeping the lead slack, entice your dog to one side with a toy or food reward. When it moves towards the reward, apply light tension to the lead. Allow the puppy to have the toy or treat, and give it copious praise.

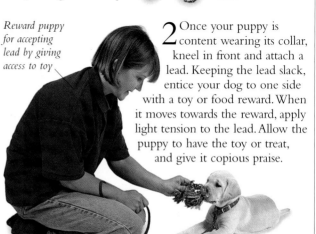

Meeting Strangers

Arrange for a canine-loving friend to meet you and your puppy outdoors. Ask your friend to kneel down to greet the puppy, as this will help curb its inclination to jump up. Also discourage direct eye contact, which can provoke an unduly excited response – not uncommon in very young dogs. Finally, provide your friend with your puppy's favourite food treat to give as a reward for relatively calm behaviour.

Prevent jumping by kneeling down rather than leaning over puppy

Essential Puppy Inoculations

Your veterinarian will vaccinate your new puppy against a range of infectious diseases, and for additional protection may also advise avoidance of unfamiliar dogs for a few weeks. Contact with known healthy dogs should continue, however, to ensure that your puppy becomes properly socialized.

Encountering Other Dogs

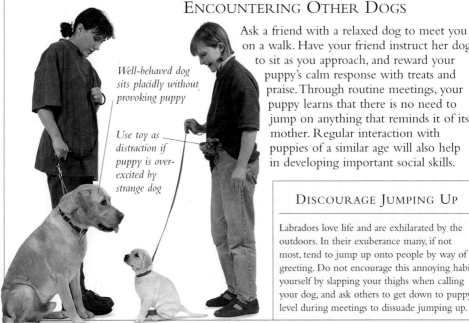

Well-behaved dog sits placidly without provoking puppy

Use toy as distraction if puppy is over-excited by strange dog

Ask a friend with a relaxed dog to meet you on a walk. Have your friend instruct her dog to sit as you approach, and reward your puppy's calm response with treats and praise. Through routine meetings, your puppy learns that there is no need to jump on anything that reminds it of its mother. Regular interaction with puppies of a similar age will also help in developing important social skills.

Discourage Jumping Up

Labradors love life and are exhilarated by the outdoors. In their exuberance many, if not most, tend to jump up onto people by way of greeting. Do not encourage this annoying habit yourself by slapping your thighs when calling your dog, and ask others to get down to puppy level during meetings to dissuade jumping up.

FIRST ROUTINES

A PUPPY'S EARLY EXPERIENCES set patterns for life. Train your young Labrador from its first days with you to accept being left alone, to wait patiently in its own crate while you are busy, and to learn about permitted behaviour. Most importantly, train it to enjoy coming to you when called.

ACCEPTING BEING LEFT ALONE

Owner walks away, giving hand signal that puppy will soon learn means "Wait"

No matter how much you enjoy being with your new puppy, there will be times when you must leave it on its own. Train your Labrador to accept that this is part of its routine by confining it to its crate with an interesting reward, such as a hollow toy filled with a little peanut butter. Then quietly walk away, signalling "Wait". Gradually accustom your dog to being left alone for extended periods.

Puppy is content in crate because it has been rewarded with exciting toy

PROBLEMS OF TRAINING SEVERAL PUPPIES

Any training requires the undivided attention of both you and your dog. If you have two or more puppies, train just one at a time, keeping the others out of sight and beyond hearing distance. Otherwise, they may actually learn not to respond to your commands since their obedience is not being reinforced. Training sessions with individual puppies should only last for a maximum of 10 minutes.

STOP OVER-AGGRESSIVE PLAY

If one puppy hurts another during rough play, the wounded puppy will usually bite back or retire from the game. Either way, the aggressive dog learns a lesson. Do the same with your puppy. If it behaves unacceptably, say "No!" and stop play for a minute. If necessary, you may grab the scruff of the neck as a firm but painless admonition.

COMING TO YOU ON COMMAND

1 For safety and responsible control, your puppy must learn always to come to you on command; this is central to all obedience. Having trained your dog to accept a collar and lead, put these on the dog and kneel a short distance away, with the lead tucked securely under one knee. Hold a chewable or attractively scented toy as a reward; a food treat is less clearly visible but may prove too exciting for many Labradors.

Appealing toy makes training fun for your dog

Puppy is distracted and ignores owner

2 Call your puppy's name in a clear, friendly tone to attract its attention. When it turns its head towards you, give the command "Come" and wave the toy as an enticement. Keep the lead slack; do not reel in your puppy but encourage it to come willingly for the reward.

When called, puppy turns and sees toy

3 Welcome your puppy with open arms. Out of curiosity, it should walk towards you. As it moves, say "Good dog" in an enthusiastic voice. When the puppy reaches you, reward it with the toy. Never call your puppy to discipline it, or it will then associate returning to you with being reprimanded. Develop a happy bond so your dog comes because it wants to be with you.

Inviting gesture and words of approval elicit response

Intrigued puppy is now alert and eager to obey command

Come, Sit, Down, Stay

TRAINING YOUR PUPPY to come, sit, lie down, and stay down is most important both for the safety of your dog and for harmonious relations with your family, friends, and outside the home. Labradors are among the most trainable of all breeds, and usually respond superbly to food rewards.

Come and Sit

1 Train only for a few minutes at a time twice daily when you, and your puppy, are alert. Try to work in a quiet, narrow space such as a hallway, with no distractions. Holding the puppy on a loose lead, briskly and cheerfully call its name and let it see that you have a food treat in your hand. As it begins to move, give the command "Come". Always be enthusiastic and encouraging. While your puppy walks towards you, praise it by saying "Good dog".

2 When your puppy reaches you, move the treat above its head. To keep its eye on the food, the puppy will naturally sit. As it does so, issue the command "Sit" and immediately give the reward. Repeat the exercise regularly until your puppy responds to words alone.

Offer reward calmly to avoid over-excitement

Lead is slack, but can be gently pulled to gain compliance

Tail held out shows puppy is not anxious or frightened while responding to command

The Value of "No!"

It is vital for everyone's well-being that your puppy quickly understands the meaning of "No!" With this one word, you can regain control and even prevent an accident. Just as you use a friendly voice and warm body language to reward, adopt a stern tone and a dominant stance when issuing this reprimand. There is no need to shout; most Labradors are exceptionally eager to please, once they know what behaviour you want. Nevertheless, it is best to practise all basic obedience commands indoors before moving outside, where your dog will be more easily diverted.

Puppy stretches along floor to receive food treat

FOLLOW DOWN

1 Kneel beside the seated puppy, holding its collar with one hand, and place the treat by its nose. If your puppy tries to get up, tuck its hindquarters under with your free hand and say "Sit". If it lunges for the food, use a less exciting reward like a soft squeaky toy.

Lead is secured under knee to maintain control

2 Move the treat forwards and down; your puppy will follow it with its nose. As it starts to lie down, give the command "Down". If the puppy refuses, gently raise the front legs into a begging position, then lower it down, rewarding its compliance with praise.

3 Still holding the collar, continue to move the food treat forwards and down until your puppy is lying completely flat. Then reward the puppy with the treat and praise. Take care not to praise excessively, as this can encourage your puppy to jump up.

Keep reward visible but held firmly until given

STAY DOWN

With practice, your Labrador should learn to stay down until commanded to rise. If it will not obey, kneel beside it and press over its shoulders. After a few seconds, release the puppy, saying "OK". Response to the "Down" command is important in potentially hazardous situations.

Place fingers gently above shoulder muscles

WALKING TO HEEL

ENSURE THAT WALKING with your dog is a pleasure rather than an endurance by teaching it from an early age to walk to heel. Labrador puppies enjoy human companionship so much that you can begin training without a lead. Then move on to lead work, gradually increasing the distance covered.

WALKING TO HEEL WITHOUT A LEAD

1 Kneel to the right of your alert, seated puppy. Holding its collar with your left hand, speak its name and show it a favourite treat in your other hand.

Owner kneels down to attract puppy's attention

2 Using the scent of the food to attract the puppy, walk in a straight line while giving the command "Heel". Be ready to grasp the collar with your left hand if the puppy wanders. When you stop walking, command "Wait".

Puppy smells treat

3 Keeping the treat low to prevent jumping, bend your knees and turn right, drawing the food round as you move. Repeat the command "Heel". Your puppy will speed up to walk round you.

Paws cross over as puppy turns to the right

4 Left turns are more difficult. Hold the collar with your left hand and command "Steady". Place the treat near your dog's mouth, then move it to the left. The puppy will follow.

Puppy moves left in pursuit of food reward

HEELWORK WITH A LEAD

1 With the puppy on a long training lead and seated to your left, hold the lead and a food treat in your right hand, and pick up the slack of the lead with your left. Tell your puppy to sit.

Tug lead gently to pull straying puppy back

Have your dog master the sequence "Sit", "Heel", "Wait"

2 Move forwards on your left foot while giving the command "Heel". If your puppy walks too far ahead, give the lead a light jerk.

3 With the puppy beside you in the heel position, offer it the reward and say "Good dog". Repeat "Sit" and praise it when it obeys.

Puppy turns to the right, keeping close to owner's leg

5 Once the right turn has been learned, commence left-turn training. Hold the treat in front of the puppy's nose to slow it down while speeding up your own circling movement to the left. Keep the puppy close and command "Steady" as it follows you round.

4 After the dog has learned to walk to heel in a straight line, teach it to turn to the right by guiding it with the treat. If your puppy has lost interest, postpone further practice until later.

Puppy slows down while concentrating intently on reward

Indoor Training

ALTHOUGH LABRADORS LOVE the outdoors, your dog is likely to spend much of its life with you in your home. Make sure that it understands basic "house rules", and provide it with its own personal space to retire to. Give your pet satisfying time and attention, but always on your own terms.

Learning to Wait Patiently

You are the leader of the pack, and you decide what happens and when. Do not respond to your dog's demands for attention or let it initiate activities. Every dog should have some private space – a bed or a crate that it can call its own. Your Labrador will learn to retire happily to its "den" while you are relaxing or busy with household chores.

Family members are uninterrupted by canine demands

Dog is content alone in comfortable bed

Spending Quality Time Together

Nurturing the bond between you and your dog is not only enjoyable, but strongly reinforces basic obedience. Set aside time each day to offer your Labrador some indoor physical and mental activity. Vary the hour and type of play, or your dog will expect a certain game at a given time.

Games keep your dog happy and alert, and are rewarding for both players

ACCEPTING STRANGERS AT HOME

Although Labradors are inclined to enjoy visitors, ensure your dog is not a nuisance by training it to sit when a guest arrives. This will discourage territorial guarding and help curb any over-excitement. Ask visitors initially to disregard your pet, to instill a sense of calm. Always reward good behaviour with approving words, a gentle stroke, or a favourite treat.

Well-behaved Labrador sits calmly, not disturbing owner and guest

RELINQUISHING A FORBIDDEN ITEM

Labradors are inveterate retrievers and often take items they find, especially those with attractive odours, back to their beds. Train your dog, using food rewards, to drop and surrender objects on command. A possessive dog should be taught that even its toys ultimately belong to you.

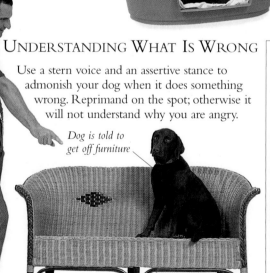

UNDERSTANDING WHAT IS WRONG

Use a stern voice and an assertive stance to admonish your dog when it does something wrong. Reprimand on the spot; otherwise it will not understand why you are angry.

Dog is told to get off furniture

FOLLOW SIMPLE RETRAINING RULES

Remember the principles of basic training and always go back to these if problems develop in adulthood. Virtually all undesirable behaviour can be corrected if your dog understands simple obedience – to come, sit, lie down, and stay. Everything else is window dressing. Labrador Retrievers are more trainable than many other breeds and have a good but limited ability to understand language. Be careful not to overload your dog with information; use short, sharp words, and issue commands only when you know that you can enforce them.

OUTSIDE THE HOME

WHETHER IN YOUR OWN GARDEN or further afield, your Labrador Retriever must be kept under secure control, both for its own protection and the safety of others. It is important to provide a healthy, hazard-free environment for your pet, and to observe social obligations conscientiously.

SHELTER AND EXERCISE

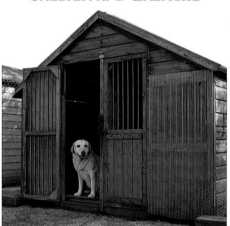

COMFORTABLE OUTDOOR KENNEL
If you plan to house your dog in a kennel, introduce it from an early age. The kennel should be chew-proof and well-insulated. Make it a cosy sanctuary, but do not keep your dog kennelled alone for long periods.

CLEAN, SPACIOUS RUN
A hygienic run attached to the kennel is ideal for several dogs, allowing fresh air and limited exercise. However, Labradors have large reserves of energy and will still need regular physical activity outside their runs.

CONTROL OUTDOORS

HALF-CHECK COLLAR
A half-check collar is often useful. Fit the collar so the soft webbing lies round your dog's throat, while the chain links sit at the back of its neck. A tug on the lead will tighten the collar without causing discomfort.

HEAD HALTER
A head halter can help with high-spirited Labradors. Ensure that it fits comfortably over the muzzle. If your dog lunges, its momentum will gently tighten the halter, pulling the head down and the jaws shut.

MUZZLE
Apply a muzzle either to obey local laws or to prevent your dog from scavenging. Use a basket variety in the correct size and properly adjusted to permit panting and barking. Never leave your muzzled dog unattended for extended lengths of time.

USING A FULL CHECK CHAIN

1 To put on a check chain correctly, hold it open in a circle as shown, then slip it round your dog's neck.

2 The chain should tighten only when the lead is pulled. If put on backwards, or if the dog is not to your left, the chain will not loosen after tension is eased.

ALWAYS GIVE PROMPT DISCIPLINE

Labrador Retrievers are lively, inquisitive dogs that, left unsupervised, may investigate further than you would like. If your dog has engaged in destructive digging, for example, reprimand it at once so that it understands why you are displeased. Enforce a lie down and stop all play; if you are away from home, return immediately. Young male Labradors in particular may need obedience reinforced when outdoors.

PLANNING A SAFE AND SECURE GARDEN

The greatest hazard presented by your garden is the risk of escape. Check that all fencing is sturdy, gate latches secure, and that hedges have no gaps. Install wire mesh where necessary. Keep all garden chemicals safely locked away, and if you have outdoor lighting, ensure that no cables are exposed and may be chewed. To prevent damage to your lawn, train your dog to use a specific site as its toilet. Be certain to store all waste and any horticultural tools securely out of reach, and do not plant material that may be poisonous to dogs. Always watch your Labrador carefully near a lit barbecue so it does not lick hot implements, and cover ornamental ponds to avoid accidents.

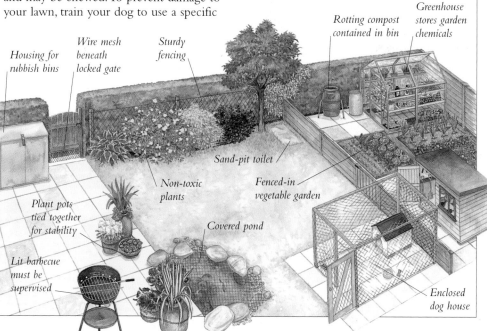

Housing for rubbish bins

Wire mesh beneath locked gate

Sturdy fencing

Rotting compost contained in bin

Greenhouse stores garden chemicals

Plant pots tied together for stability

Non-toxic plants

Sand-pit toilet

Fenced-in vegetable garden

Lit barbecue must be supervised

Covered pond

Enclosed dog house

TRAVEL AND BOARDING

WITH PROPER CARE, your Labrador should happily accept both routine travel and regular holidays. Introduce car journeys as early as possible, and make trips safe and enjoyable. Closely monitor your dog when in new surroundings, and ensure that it will be secure and comfortable if left with others while you are away.

HOLIDAYS WITH OR WITHOUT YOUR DOG

PREPARING FOR A TRIP

Labradors are good travellers and willingly go almost anywhere. On trips, take your dog's food and water bowls, collar, lead, and bedding, and add holiday contact addresses or telephone numbers to its name tag. At your destination, find a local veterinarian who can deal with any emergencies.

Purpose-made rucksack allows dog to carry its own light load

HOME AWAY FROM HOME

Ask your vet's advice about kennelling your dog. Visit recommended establishments and inspect their housing and runs for cleanliness and security. Ask how often your dog will be exercised or played with each day, and satisfy yourself that the staff are responsible. Dogs that are introduced to kennels early in life take revisits in their stride. Before kennelling, ensure that your dog's health inoculations are up to date. Dog-sitting services are another alternative; again, your vet can offer guidance.

BE CONSIDERATE OF OTHERS

Local dog-control regulations vary; wherever you are, observe any relevant notices. Never exercise your Labrador in restricted areas, and obey laws specifying that dogs must be kept under control or on leads, especially in parks and on beaches. Always clean up after your dog. Carry a supply of plastic bags, or use a "poop scoop", and deposit mess in special waste bins if available. Control your dog, and do not let it be a nuisance to others.

SAFE TRAVELLING BY CAR

CANINE SEATBELT
Your Labrador risks the same injuries that you do in a car accident. A dog can travel safely on the rear seat of a car if secured with a special canine seatbelt which, like a child's harness, attaches to the standard seatbelt anchors. With this device, the dog is kept reassuringly in place and under control, so that it cannot distract the driver.

ADDED SECURITY IN CRATE
Professional dog handlers prefer to transport their dogs in crates. These are roomy and secure, and help keep your car free from dog hair or chewing damage. Introduce your Labrador to its crate during puppyhood, as its regular bed and playpen in the home. Then, when the crate is used as transport, your dog will be inclined to relax and enjoy the journey. If it becomes over-excited, install sunblinds as screening. On long trips, stop every few hours to allow your dog to exercise, drink, and relieve itself.

PROTECTIVE REAR GRILLE
If your dog is to be transported in the back of an estate car, ensure that it has comfortable bedding. Install a purpose-made dog grille to deter your Labrador from jumping into the rear seat. Fit the grille securely so that in the event of a sudden stop it will act as a guard, preventing your dog from hurtling forwards.

HOT CARS ARE DEATHTRAPS

Heatstroke is one of the most common causes of preventable death in dogs. A dog cannot sweat other than through its pads; therefore excess body heat can be reduced only by panting. In hot conditions, the body temperature rises quickly, sometimes within minutes, and if there is no escape a dog can die. Never leave your dog in your car, even parked in the shade or with the windows slightly open, in warm or sunny weather. In cold weather, do not leave your dog in brilliant sunshine with the car engine running and the heater on high. It can be just as lethal.

CONSTRUCTIVE PLAY

DOGS NEED MENTAL STIMULATION as well as physical exercise. Create activities that utilize the Labrador's unique abilities; games involving retrieving will be particularly enjoyable for your dog. Use playtime to reinforce training, to strengthen your bond as owner, and simply to have fun.

Most Labradors naturally hold items without dropping them

CHALLENGING GAMES

Simple rehearsed scenarios such as supplying a handkerchief on the command of a "sneeze" are an enjoyable way of developing your dog's ability to recognize a given cue and react accordingly. This type of game exploits the Labrador's love of both retrieving and social interaction.

"Achoo" becomes the cue to fetch

Dog "finds" handkerchief in pocket

FETCHING USEFUL ITEMS

Labradors instinctively retrieve, and will happily bring almost anything to you. Train your dog to fetch your slippers by throwing one a short distance and saying "Fetch", followed by "Come". Use a lead first to ensure response to the command.

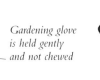

Gardening glove is held gently and not chewed

RETRIEVING ON DEMAND

Once your dog understands the concept of fetching, you can train it to find any item. It must, however, be taught to understand exactly what you want it to bring back. Do not expect your Labrador to fetch something it has not been specifically trained to retrieve.

ENJOYABLE LEARNED ROUTINES

Physical games are the most exciting for your dog, but even "playing dead" can be satisfying when rewarded with treats or praise. This entertaining set piece is an extension of the "Down" command, with your dog learning to lie still until you release it by saying "OK".

Pointed fingers and signal "Bang" start the action

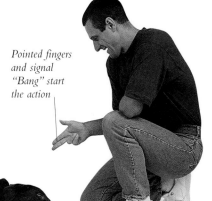

Dog obligingly "collapses" in response

HAVING FUN WITH MOVING OBJECTS

Labradors are moderately good soccer players, although they usually lack the desire to win that some terriers have! Giving verbal encouragement, teach your dog to roll a ball with its nose. Avoid food rewards as these are too potent a distraction from the game.

TOYS BELONG TO YOU

When you finish playing, make a point of putting away all toys. This re-establishes that you are in charge, and playtime is available only through you. It also makes toys more desirable to your dog, and therefore more useful to you as a control tool. Always give praise for relinquishing toys, or exchange them for a food reward.

Toy is surrendered gladly for treat

END PLAYING WITH REWARDS AND PRAISE

Constructive games keep your dog's mind active and alert. Adequate mental as well as physical exercise can help prevent destructiveness or anxiety, which are often merely symptoms of boredom. It is easy to incorporate training into play by continually reinforcing basic obedience commands such as "Sit", "Stay", "Come", and "Down", and by rewarding good behaviour. Always finish games on a positive note, with food treats, stroking, or encouraging words, so that your Labrador looks forward to future activities. Just as with children, if learning is fun, dogs will want to learn more.

GOOD CONTROL

THE LABRADOR RETRIEVER is the world's most popular family dog, but even a Labrador can develop unacceptable behaviour. Some problems are rooted in natural instincts, while others may arise from inadequate attention. Most difficulties can be overcome through positive control.

RESISTING TEMPTATION

Labradors will grab any chance of a snack. Prevent begging by never giving food while you are eating. Relenting occasionally will strongly reinforce this habit. If your dog begs, command it to lie down, then look away.

Well-trained dog knows it cannot have child's ice-cream

Dog chews toy contentedly while owner is away

HAPPILY OCCUPIED ALONE

Labradors tend to dislike being left alone, and separation anxiety or boredom can result in destructive behaviour. Always leave and return without a fuss, and exercise and feed your dog before you go out, to encourage rest. Provide a favourite toy for quiet entertainment.

Maintain control with lead for first meeting

Friend's easy-going dog is used as the "stooge"

MAKING NEW CANINE FRIENDS

Most Labradors enjoy meeting other dogs. Females are rarely hostile, but may be slightly apprehensive. Socialize your pet through arranged meetings with dogs that are well controlled. Keep both dogs on a lead for the initial introduction. After they have sniffed each other thoroughly to become acquainted, allow play if circumstances permit.

Dog remains calm as girl passes by on skateboard

ACCEPTING NEW SITUATIONS

Labradors are generally curious about strange or unusual situations, but may react nervously to common yet unexpected objects such as baby strollers, umbrellas, or children's toys like skateboards. If your dog is alarmed by a new sight or sound, re-present the stimulus from a distance that does not provoke distress and reward composure. Over time, reduce the distance, always rewarding calm acceptance.

DEALING WITH A WILFUL DOG

Wilfulness can take many forms. Labradors may be territorial, fiercely protecting their homes and possessions. Some males are aggressive only towards fellow males, while others look for any opportunity to dominate and hence move up the pecking order towards leadership of the pack. With all aggressive behaviour, it is essential to understand what type of antagonism your dog is showing before tackling the problem. In virtually all circumstances, you must firmly establish your own position of respect.

DETERRENTS FOR CHEWING

Bored Labradors are diligent chewers, but usually indulge in this when you are not around. Be creative, and plan for discipline to take place in your absence by spraying an article that is likely to be chewed with a safe but bitter-tasting aerosol. Trainers call this aversion therapy; it is highly effective because the dog teaches itself.

Bitter spray, available from pet stores, can deter chewing

Lead itself may incite dog to pull; tugging back will be seen as a game

Labrador lunges forwards eagerly, forgetting training to walk to heel

LEARNING NOT TO LUNGE

The typical Labrador is enthusiastic, particularly about the outdoors, and may pull on its lead with excitement. If this occurs, return to basic training. Reinforce the commands "Sit" and "Down", then retrain walking to heel, both on and off the lead. If your dog is particularly strong-willed, consider using a head halter.

FOODS FOR YOUR DOG

AS A BREED, THE LABRADOR RETRIEVER has been dubbed the "walking stomach". If your Labrador refuses to eat, it is time to call your vet. Choose from commercial and home-prepared foods to meet dietary needs and personal tastes, but remember that you control what your dog eats, not the dog.

CANNED FOODS

Moist, meaty canned foods come in a wide range of flavours and textures to satisfy your Labrador's appetite. High in protein, they are usually mixed with dry dog meal to add calories and vital carbohydrates. Canned foods are nutritious and tasty, but will not stay fresh in the bowl for more than a few hours.

Standard variety

Special formula for clinical conditions

"Stew" with gravy

Chunks in jelly

DRY MEAL

Crunchy dry meal is added to canned food to improve the texture, contribute fibre and fat, as well as exercise the jaws.

COMPLETE DRY FOODS

Complete dry foods are well-balanced and convenient to store in bulk. Concentrated, they contain about four times the calories of canned foods, so a dog needs smaller quantities. There are varieties to suit all ages and for specific needs, including weight control or medical conditions such as bowel inflammation or impaired kidney function.

HIGH-ENERGY
Puppies require nutrient-rich, easily-digestible foods to sustain growth.

REGULAR
Adult formulas maintain mature dogs on a variety of activity levels.

LOW-CALORIE
Older, overweight, or sedentary dogs need less energy from their food.

TEETH-CLEANING
These large, crunchy chunks promote healthy gums and help control tartar.

SEMI-MOIST FOODS

These foods are packaged in many flavours, even cheese, and have three times the calories of canned foods. A high carbohydrate content makes semi-moist foods unsuitable for diabetic dogs. Like dry foods, they can be left out all day to be eaten at leisure – although Labradors are rarely so picky!

SUITABLE CHEWS

Labradors need large, hard chews to work their teeth and massage the gums. Avoid small chews that may be swallowed, or sterilized bones which can break teeth.

Rawhide chew

TREATS AND BISCUITS

It is fun to give your dog snack foods, but remember that many are high in calories and can lead to obesity. Offer snacks as rewards, not on demand, and limit the amount given daily. The more your Labrador receives, the smaller its regular meals should be.

MIXED ASSORTMENT   MARROWBONE   BEEF BONE SHAPES   CHEESE-FLAVOURED

TABLE FOODS

In general, a diet that is well-balanced for us is also nourishing for canines. Never encourage begging by feeding scraps from the table, but prepare a special portion for your dog consisting of equal parts meat and vegetables, pasta, or rice. Avoid strong spices.

Dogs, like humans, are omnivores and can be given meat, starch, and vegetables

LIGHT MEALS

Labradors enjoy routine and are content with the same food each day. However, an occasional change is fine as long as it is easily digested. Breakfast cereals and bread are good ingredients for a light meal.

Cereal with milk is a good source of roughage and vitamins

HEALTHY EATING

A NUTRITIOUS DIET and sound eating habits are essential to good health. Provide the right foods in the correct quantity for your dog's needs, and plenty of fresh water to prevent dehydration. Since most Labradors love to eat, avert begging or obesity by feeding at set times.

DIETARY NEEDS FOR ALL AGES

GROWING PUPPY

Puppies need plenty of nutrients for healthy growth. Up to 12 weeks of age, feed your puppy four times daily. Reduce this to three meals until it is six months old, then provide two meals a day through to the first year.

Bowl has non-slip bottom for easier eating

Serve food at room temperature, never straight from refrigerator

MATURE ADULT

The dietary requirements of an adult dog vary enormously, depending upon its health, activity levels, and temperament. Feed twice daily to appease your Labrador's stomach, but refer any obvious weight gain to your vet.

WAITING FOR FOOD

It is important to establish a strict routine for mealtimes. Train your dog to sit and wait in the presence of food and to eat only when released to do so. Always give food in the dog's own bowl, and never offer titbits while you are eating. Without proper control, Labradors are inclined to beg shamelessly.

In response to "Stay" command, dog waits patiently for signal to eat

Sixteen-year-old prefers to take its meals lying down

ELDERLY LABRADOR

Older, as well as neutered, dogs have lower energy demands and should be fed smaller portions or less calorie-rich foods. Protein intake may be reduced to help prevent obesity, which places undue strain on the hind legs and organs such as the kidneys.

DAILY ENERGY DEMANDS FOR ALL STAGES OF LIFE

AGE	WEIGHT	CALORIES	DRY FOOD	SEMI-MOIST	CANNED/MEAL
2 MONTHS	5 kg (11 lb)	1,120	335 g (12 oz)	380 g (13 oz)	555 g/190 g (20 oz/7 oz)
3 MONTHS	10 kg (22 lb)	1,645	480 g (17 oz)	530 g (19 oz)	825 g/285 g (29 oz/10 oz)
6 MONTHS	25 kg (55 lb)	2,325	700 g (25 oz)	765 g (27 oz)	1165 g/395 g (41 oz/14 oz)
TYPICAL ADULT	26–43 kg (57–95 lb)	1,265–1,850	380–555 g (13–20 oz)	425–630 g (15–22 oz)	630–925 g/215–300 g (22–33 oz/8–11 oz)
ACTIVE ADULT	26–43 kg (57–95 lb)	1,440–2,100	425–630 g (15–22 oz)	480–700 g (17–25 oz)	700–1050 g/265–380 g (25–37 oz/9–13 oz)
VERY ACTIVE ADULT	26–43 kg (57–95 lb)	2,015–2,940	595–880 g (21–31 oz)	670–980 g (24–35 oz)	1010–1470 g/335–500 g (36–52 oz/12–18 oz)
ELDERLY (10 YEARS+)	26–43 kg (57–95 lb)	1,150–1,680	335–500 g (12–18 oz)	385–555 g (14–20 oz)	555–840 g/190–285 g (20–30 oz/7–10 oz)

FEEDING REQUIREMENTS

These figures represent an approximate guide only. Remember that each dog has its own specific nutritional needs, and that different brands of food vary in calories.

Always provide a well-balanced diet to meet your dog's daily energy requirements. If you are uncertain of what is best for your Labrador, seek detailed professional advice.

CHAMPION SCAVENGERS

The Labrador "radar" for food is quite uncanny. Scavenging can become a habit if rewarded with success; prevent this by securing all rubbish and keeping tempting items out of reach. In its quest to seek and devour, your dog may eagerly swallow inedible or damaging objects; therefore teach it from an early age to drop articles on command. Control chronic scavenging with either a long training lead or a muzzle.

Single-minded male cannot resist raiding full dustbin

CONTROLLING AN UNSAVOURY APPETITE

Labradors have a rather unrefined palate, and may be attracted to the most repugnant refuse. Outdoors, they will quickly sniff out animal droppings, and regard them as dessert! This is natural behaviour, and horse, rabbit, or deer faeces can actually be nourishing for dogs. Eating canine droppings, however, may cause intestinal ailments. Tell your dog "No", and make it drop any excrement it picks up. A spice-treated stool is also a good deterrent.

BASIC BODY CARE

GOOD NATURAL ANATOMY and a protective coat mean that routine maintenance for Labradors is minimal. A hunting dog by nature, much of the general wear and tear arises from running around, jumping in and out of water, and rolling in the mud. Check the cleanliness of all body openings daily.

ENSURING CLEAR, HEALTHY EYES

Healthy eyes are bright and sparkling with dull pink mucous membranes. Some older Labradors have droopy lower eyelids which allow debris to collect, causing inflammation. Bathe the area around your dog's eyes daily with cotton wool moistened with tepid salt water. If the eyes appear reddened or cloudy, or show any discharge or signs of squinting, contact your veterinarian to arrange a thorough examination.

Dampen cotton wool to avoid loose fibres

BRUSHING THE TEETH

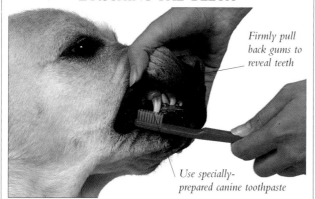

Firmly pull back gums to reveal teeth

Use specially-prepared canine toothpaste

Check daily for any items lodged in the mouth or between the teeth. Once a week clean the teeth, avoiding human toothpaste as it froths and will be swallowed. Use an up-and-down motion with a soft brush to massage the gums.

PREVENT TARTAR

Without routine cleaning, tartar can accumulate on the teeth, leading to bad breath, root infection, and gum disease. In addition to regular professional scaling, rawhide chews are helpful in controlling tartar build-up. This Labrador's teeth and gums require medical attention.

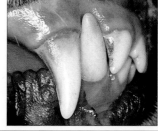

INSPECTING THE EARS

Examine the ears daily for foreign material such as grass seeds, and for inflammation, wax, or odour. Remove excess wax carefully with a dampened tissue; a cotton bud can act like a plunger and push wax further into the ear.

CUTTING THE NAILS

Clip after bathing, when nails are soft and pliable

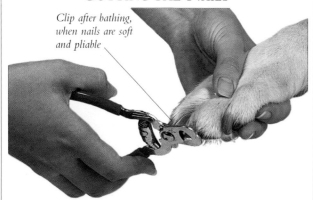

A Labrador's nails seldom need clipping. If they do grow long, command your dog to sit and use a non-crushing "guillotine" clipper. Yellow Labradors' pink nails are the easiest to trim, as the quick is clearly visible. With black or chocolate dogs, take extra care to avoid this sensitive area.

WHERE TO CLIP NAILS

The pink interior, called the quick or nail bed, contains blood vessels and nerves. Always cut in front of the quick. If unsure, ask your vet to demonstrate the correct technique.

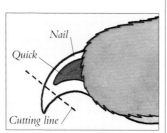

Nail

Quick

Cutting line

WASHING THE PAWS

Wash dirt off the paws with tepid or cool water, rubbing your fingers between the pads to remove hardened mud. Avoid hot water, especially in cold weather, and only use cleansers safe for human skin. Rinse and dry the paws thoroughly afterwards.

ANAL HYGIENE

Excessive licking or dragging of the rear can mean that the scent-producing anal sacs are blocked, causing discomfort. Wearing protective gloves, squeeze the sacs empty, applying firm pressure from both sides. Use absorbent material to collect the fluid.

MAINTAINING THE COAT

WITH THEIR SHORT, DENSE COATS, Labradors are relatively simple to groom and rarely need their hair trimmed. Nevertheless, they moult extensively and demand some attention at least weekly. The Labrador is also a first-class muck-roller, so regular bathing will prove inevitable.

ROUTINE GROOMING

THOROUGH BRUSHING
Command your dog to sit or stand. A bristle brush will remove dead hair and debris, as well as massage the skin. If using a double-surfaced brush, take care with the pin side, which can be harsh on delicate skin if applied too vigorously.

Brush with natural lay of hair

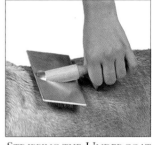

STRIPPING THE UNDERCOAT
Use a slicker brush during heavy moults to clear the large quantities of woolly, insulating undercoat. Always check for signs of parasites or other skin irritations.

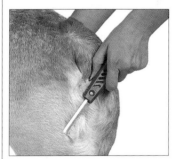

COMBING OUT DEAD HAIR
A comb is needed only in cold weather, when Labradors have a thick double coat. Concentrate on the hips, thighs, and tail, where dead hair accumulates. Comb thoroughly, but avoid scratching the skin.

SHINING THE COAT
Complete the grooming routine by smoothing the coat with a clean, dry chamois leather. This wipes any loose flakes of skin from the surface and creates a glossy sheen. Let your dog know that grooming is finished by giving the release command "OK", then reward its obedience with verbal praise.

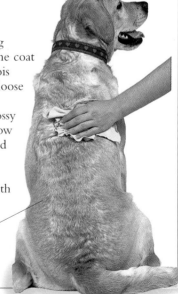

Most Labradors find grooming extremely enjoyable

MOULTING CARE

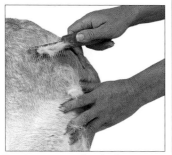

During your Labrador's twice-yearly moults, it is advisable to groom at least twice a week. If neglected, elderly dogs in particular can develop matts of moulted hair over the hips and at the base of the tail.

ESTABLISH GROOMING AS A BASIC RITUAL

In canine terms, grooming represents an act of dominance, taking most dogs back to puppyhood, when they were dependent on their mothers to keep them clean. Labradors usually love to be groomed, but some naturally strong-willed individuals, especially males, may resent it. To avoid such problems, introduce grooming routines as soon as you acquire your dog. It will quickly learn to accept your actions as a sign of leadership, and should comply contentedly.

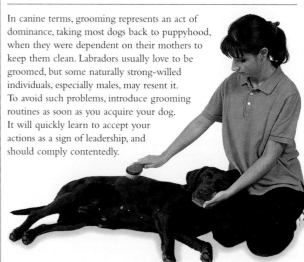

BATHING YOUR DOG

1 Although Labradors generally love to get wet, they are less happy being washed. Keep a firm grip on your dog (or enlist a helper) and use a non-slip mat in the bath for safety. Lather thoroughly with dog or baby shampoo and tepid to warm water. Bathe outdoors with a garden hose only in hot weather.

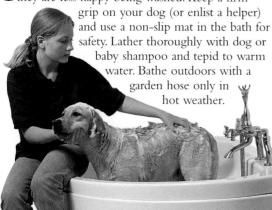

2 After washing, rinse off all the shampoo, removing any residual deposits from under the legs and tail. Avoid getting shampoo near the eyes or water in the ears. Continually talk to your dog in a firm but gentle tone while bathing.

3 After rinsing, squeeze excess water from the coat and wrap your dog in a towel. Let it shake, then vigorously rub its coat dry or use a hairdryer set to warm, not hot. A typical Labrador will now be eager to roll around to get rid of the artificial shampoo odour. It might smell fresh to you, but your dog still prefers the aroma of dead fish!

BASIC HEALTH

YOUR LABRADOR DEPENDS on you for its good health. Since it cannot tell you that something is wrong, you must observe how your dog moves and behaves; any changes in activity or regular habits may be warning signs of problems. Arrange annual check-ups, and always use your vet as a source of advice.

EASY, GRACEFUL MOVEMENT

Healthy dogs walk, trot, and run freely and effortlessly. A Labrador should move with fluidity and ease, its legs strong, straight, and true. A ponderous gait can be caused by excess weight, while difficulties lying down or getting up may indicate joint problems – not uncommon, especially in older dogs. Limping is a sign that one leg in particular hurts, and head bobbing while walking usually also means that a dog is in pain. Watch your dog in its daily activities and be alert to any discomfort or loss of mobility.

SOUND APPETITE AND EATING HABITS

Eating and toilet routines adopted during puppyhood are normally maintained throughout life. Even slight changes can be a sign of ill health, and should be referred to your vet. A reduced appetite is very uncommon in Labradors, and although it can simply indicate boredom, it may also signal illness. Asking for food but not eating it can mean tooth pain. So too can sloppy eating – with food being dropped, then picked up and eaten. Occasionally, Labradors will "eat" inedible items such as pebbles or soil. This can be learned behaviour,

but may reflect a digestive disorder or mineral deficiency. A heightened appetite without weight gain can indicate a thyroid problem. Increased thirst is always important and may be a sign of infection or conditions such as diabetes and liver or kidney disease.

Excessive drinking is medically significant

ACTIVE AND ALERT?

Canines are creatures of habit. If your dog does not get up when it usually does, moves slower, or is reluctant to play, it could be ill. However, because Labradors are stoic and relish human companionship, they will often try to behave normally to please their owner, even when unwell. Observe your dog closely; if its actions seem even slightly strange, consult your veterinarian for advice.

CARING FOR THE OLDER DOG

Do not expect your dog to remain puppy-like forever. With age, it will slow down and may become hard of hearing, even irritable at times. Be patient with its behaviour, and gentle in your handling. Try to create less physically demanding activities; elderly dogs still enjoy playing, but are less agile and energetic. Given as part of the daily diet, a tennis ball cut with a hole and filled with dry food offers excellent mental stimulation to help keep your Labrador young at heart.

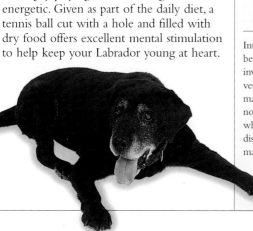

REGULAR HEALTH CHECKS

Using stethoscope, vet listens to heart and lung sounds

Labrador sits comfortably on table and is content to be examined

Dogs that are vaccinated and have annual health check-ups tend to live longer than those that do not. Many conditions, such as splenic tumours, are not outwardly apparent, but may be diagnosed upon close physical examination. Always inform your vet of any observed deviations in behaviour; problems are easiest to treat if detected early. Later in your Labrador's life, regular twice-yearly clinic visits may be recommended.

MAKING VISITS TO THE VET FUN

Introduce your Labrador to the veterinary clinic before it needs any treatment, so that it can have an investigative sniff and explore the premises. Ask your vet to give your dog a food treat while it is there, to make the next visit more appealing. If your vet does not supply treats, take some yourself and offer them when your dog is inoculated; this will provide suitable distraction from the unpleasant. Repeat trips can be made less of a hardship for you, too, by taking out insurance cover on your pet's health. This will ensure that you can benefit from the most sophisticated diagnostics and treatments.

COMMON PROBLEMS

ALL DOGS ARE PRONE to internal and external parasites, although serious gastrointestinal conditions are rare in this inveterate scavenger. Labradors' lopped ears, however, can lead to regular infections, while their love of chewing causes more tooth fractures than seen in smaller breeds.

SKIN PARASITES

Labradors, particularly working ones, contract fleas, ticks, lice, and mites from other dogs and wildlife. Always check your dog's coat thoroughly when returning from the countryside.

FLEA INFESTATION
This common parasite injects saliva when it bites, causing skin irritation and scratching. Use flea-control methods recommended by your vet.

TICK-BORNE DISEASE
Ticks, carried by sheep and deer, may transmit infectious diseases. Visible to the eye, they can be killed with a dab of alcohol and removed with a quick twist.

TYPICAL CANINE COMPLAINTS

With any breed, many health problems can be prevented. Routinely inspect your dog's skin, ears, and teeth, and keep all vaccinations up to date. If heartworm is a threat in your area, provide appropriate medication as directed.

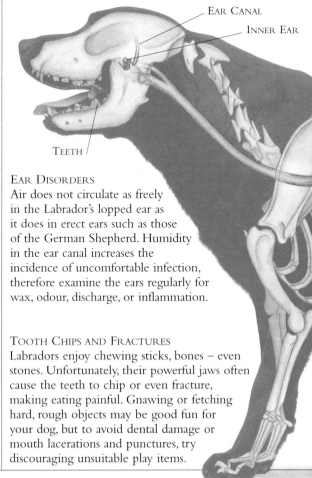

EAR CANAL

INNER EAR

TEETH

EAR DISORDERS
Air does not circulate as freely in the Labrador's lopped ear as it does in erect ears such as those of the German Shepherd. Humidity in the ear canal increases the incidence of uncomfortable infection, therefore examine the ears regularly for wax, odour, discharge, or inflammation.

TOOTH CHIPS AND FRACTURES
Labradors enjoy chewing sticks, bones – even stones. Unfortunately, their powerful jaws often cause the teeth to chip or even fracture, making eating painful. Gnawing or fetching hard, rough objects may be good fun for your dog, but to avoid dental damage or mouth lacerations and punctures, try discouraging unsuitable play items.

OBVIOUS SIGNS OF DISCOMFORT

PERSISTENT LICKING

All dogs lick to groom themselves, but Labradors in particular may do so obsessively, causing skin inflammation and hair loss. Called "lick granuloma", this exaggerated grooming disorder often responds well to anti-anxiety drugs.

Itchy skin is not always caused by parasites

Excessive licking of hind paw

SCRATCHING

Dogs often scratch because of parasites, but allergies or injuries can be additional causes. Always have any irritation checked by your vet, who will prescribe suitable treatment, which may include anti-inflammatory drugs, antibiotics, medicated shampoos, dietary changes, and varied grooming.

LIVER

KIDNEY

SPLEEN

INTESTINES

JOINT DISEASE

Joints are vulnerable if a young dog carries too much weight during its growth phase. Hips, knees, hocks, and ankles can become inflamed, leading to painful arthritis. Prevent this with routine exercise and a healthy diet.

TAIL BONE

PAINFUL STRAINS

Your Labrador's muscles, tendons, and ligaments are designed to support an active dog at optimum weight. Obesity often leads to injuries, as can excessively vigorous exercise in normally sedentary dogs. Torn knee ligaments is a serious injury most commonly found in older, overweight Labradors. Unfortunately, it is a complex condition requiring surgery.

STOMACH

KNEE JOINT

INTESTINAL PARASITES

Intestinal worms and other internal parasites may cause weight loss, vomiting, or diarrhoea with or without blood and mucus. A dull coat, bloated abdomen, or chronic dragging of the hindquarters can indicate worms. Consult your vet on effective worm prevention.

BREED-SPECIFIC PROBLEMS

SELECTIVE BREEDING FOR DESIRABLE traits inevitably also concentrates potentially harmful genes. Like all other breeds, the Labrador has its own variety of inherited medical problems. The primary clinical conditions involve the joints, eyes, and brain, with obesity often an additional problem.

HIP DYSPLASIA

Although partly hereditary, this condition can also be related to excessive weight or over-vigorous exercise during puppyhood. Signs of hip dysplasia include thigh muscle wasting and discomfort on rising. In severe cases, dogs "bunny hop" to diminish pain. Veterinary associations and kennel clubs have developed useful hip-testing schemes.

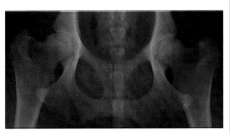

NORMAL HIPS
The hip is a basic ball-and-socket joint. In healthy hips like these, the head of the femur (ball) sits comfortably and firmly in the acetabulum (socket) of the hip bone.

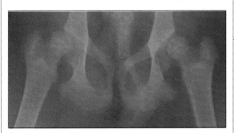

DYSPLASTIC JOINTS
This X-ray of a Labrador with severe hip dysplasia shows shallow, rough hip sockets and abrasive femoral heads. Any movement of one against the other causes pain.

HEREDITARY EYE DISEASES

Labrador Retrievers can suffer from a variety of inherited eye ailments. Breeding stock should have their eyes routinely examined for detached retinas, cataracts, and any signs of diseases such as entropion, retinal dysplasia, and progressive retinal atrophy – a later-life blindness in which the retina "dies". It will soon be possible through DNA blood "fingerprinting" (as it already is with Irish Setters) to detect individual carriers of the genes that cause hereditary eye disorders.

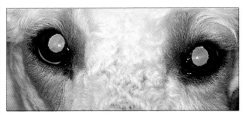

CLOUDING OF THE LENSES
This dog has cataracts, with obvious loss of transparency of the crystalline lens in each eye. The condition is painless, but clarity of vision is severely impaired.

IMPORTANCE OF HEALTH SCREENING

All conscientious breeders participate in accredited screening programmes, often jointly run by kennel clubs and veterinary associations, and will be able to provide relevant certificates stating that a dog is clear of inherited eye disorders, and giving a comparative rating for any hip abnormalities. In a number of countries, anatomical, behavioural, and hereditary factor surveys are carried out by breed clubs, with dogs classified as "recommended for breeding", "suitable for breeding", or "not suitable".

OTHER DISORDERS COMMON IN LABRADORS

Although Labradors generally have robust constitutions and sound physiques, they are nevertheless susceptible to certain medical conditions. Some are inherited and cannot be prevented, but treatment may help to alleviate symptoms. Always keep your dog at a healthy weight; with their stocky build and hearty appetite, Labradors can easily become obese.

OSTEOCHONDROSIS
This increasingly diagnosed disease, in which areas of joint cartilage "die", is particularly prevalent in the larger breeds, and usually first affects puppies between four and eight months old. It may occur in any joint, but Labradors suffer most frequently in the elbows, showing pain-induced lameness, leading to arthritis in later life. Implicated causal factors are genetic make-up, hormone imbalance, diet, exercise, and growth rate. Treatment for the condition, identified by X-ray, often involves surgery.

DEAFNESS AND EPILEPSY
Deafness is not uncommon in elderly Labradors, as nerve transmission to the brain gradually deteriorates. Epilepsy, another inherited condition, although far rarer, is distressing for both you and your dog, and requires veterinary attention.

BRAIN

OESOPHAGUS

SPINAL COLUMN

INTESTINES

LARYNX

TRACHEA

ELBOW JOINT

"DEPRAVED" APPETITE
Labradors love food, and can sometimes develop a "depraved" appetite, trademarked by the eating of faeces. This distasteful habit may be caused by an enzyme deficiency. If so, supplement the diet with papain-rich pineapple, papaya, pumpkin, or vegetable marrow.

STOMACH

LARYNGEAL PARALYSIS
Incidence of this old-age illness is higher in Labradors than in all other breeds combined. Its symptoms are very obvious: loud, distressed breathing, coughing, and a muted bark. It is caused by the larynx (voice box) collapsing over the windpipe, reducing air supply; the only cure is by surgical correction.

FORESEEING DANGERS

OUR DAILY SURROUNDINGS can present many dangers for a dog. Be mindful of your Labrador's natural inclinations, and supervise it closely – especially outdoors – to prevent mishaps. Never leave your dog alone in situations where it may imperil itself or others, and be prepared to avert and react to trouble.

ENSURING SAFETY WITH YOUR LIVELY LABRADOR

DEALING WITH BOISTEROUS BEHAVIOUR
An ebullient Labrador can unwittingly injure someone or cause property damage. If your dog accidentally or intentionally bites, both you and your pet may face legal redress. Good training is a social duty as well as sound prevention, but also obtain insurance for your dog's activities.

POTENTIAL HAZARDS IN WATER
Labradors are marvellous swimmers, but treacherous or icy waters should still be avoided. Be wary of water-borne diseases such as leptospirosis, spread by infected rat urine, and blue-green algae bloom, which can cause itchy skin, diarrhoea, and even death. Ensure that your dog will be able to safely get in, and out of, any body of water.

CONTROLLING AN INQUISITIVE NATURE
Monitor your Labrador carefully when off the lead. Impetuous, curious dogs are more prone to injury, and exploratory wanders or investigative digging can result in bites from wild animals, stings, and irritations caused by plants or insects. Keep your dog away from known dangers, and carry a first-aid kit to treat minor cuts and lacerations. Always use a lead to maintain firm control whenever your dog or others may be at risk.

COMMON POISONS AND CONTAMINANTS

IF INGESTED		ACTION
Slug and snail bait Strychnine rat poison two Illegal drugs Aspirin and other painkillers Sedatives and antidepressants	Warfarin rat poison Lead (batteries, etc.) Antifreeze	Examine the package and determine its contents. If the poison was swallowed within the last two hours, induce vomiting by giving crystals of washing soda, a "ball" of wet salt, or 3% hydrogen peroxide by mouth. Consult your vet immediately.
Caustic soda Dishwasher granules Paint remover or thinner Kerosene or petrol Drain, toilet, or oven cleaner	Chlorine bleach Laundry detergents Wood preservatives Polishes	Do not induce vomiting. Give raw egg white, bicarbonate of soda, charcoal powder, or olive oil by mouth. Apply a paste of bicarbonate of soda to any burns in the mouth. Seek urgent medical advice from your veterinarian.

IF IN CONTACT WITH THE COAT	ACTION
Paint Tar Petroleum products Motor oil	Do not apply paint remover or concentrated biological detergents. Wearing protective gloves, rub plenty of liquid paraffin or vegetable oil into the coat. Bathe with warm, soapy water or baby shampoo. Rub in flour to help absorb the poison.
Anything other than paint, tar, petroleum products, and motor oil	Wearing protective gloves, flush the affected area for at least five minutes, using plenty of clean, tepid water. Then bathe the contaminated coat thoroughly with warm, soapy water or mild, non-irritating baby shampoo.

EMERGENCY TREATMENT

With any case of poisoning, look for signs of shock, and give essential first aid as required. Contact your vet or local poison-control centre for specific advice, and begin home treatment as quickly as possible, preferably under professional guidance by telephone.

STORE ALL TOXINS SECURELY

Labrador Retrievers, especially when young, are inveterate chewers. Keep all household, garden, and swimming-pool chemicals stored safely out of reach, and never give your dog an empty container as a toy, or it will regard all similar objects as play items – with potentially tragic results.

PROTECTION FROM ELECTRICAL HAZARDS

Puppies naturally gnaw anything, and often find the texture of electric flex particularly appealing. Train your dog from an early age not to tamper with electrical apparatus, and reduce the risk of burns or electrocution by placing electrical cords out of reach or spraying them with bitter-tasting aerosol. Switch off sockets when not in use and, if possible, add protective covers. If your Labrador does chew through a live cable, do not risk your own life. Turn off the main electricity supply before administering first aid.

EMERGENCY FIRST AID

A HOME FIRST-AID KIT IS ESSENTIAL for patching up minor injuries. More serious emergencies are thankfully much less common, but with an understanding of basic principles and techniques such as artificial respiration and cardiac massage, you could save your dog's life.

FIRST-AID PRINCIPLES AND BASIC EQUIPMENT

The fundamentals of human first aid also apply to dogs. Your objectives are to preserve life, prevent further injury, control damage, minimize pain and distress, promote healing, and get your dog safely to a veterinarian for professional care. Have a fully-stocked first-aid kit handy and use it to treat minor wounds, once you are certain there are no more serious, life-threatening problems to deal with.

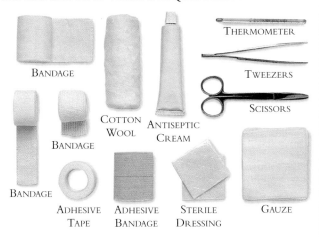

BANDAGE

BANDAGE

BANDAGE

COTTON WOOL

ADHESIVE TAPE

ADHESIVE BANDAGE

ANTISEPTIC CREAM

STERILE DRESSING

THERMOMETER

TWEEZERS

SCISSORS

GAUZE

HOW TO ASSESS AN UNCONSCIOUS DOG

Causes of unconsciousness include choking, electrocution, blood loss, near-drowning, poisoning, concussion, shock, fainting, smoke inhalation, diabetes, and heart failure. If you find your dog apparently unconscious, call its name to see if it responds. Pinch hard between the toes, while checking the eyes for blinking. Pull on a limb – does your dog pull back? Put your hand firmly on its chest and feel for a heartbeat. Lift the lip and look at the colour of the gums. If they are pink and when you squeeze the pinkness out it comes back immediately, your dog's heart is beating. If the gums are pale or blue, cardiac massage may be required to restore circulation.

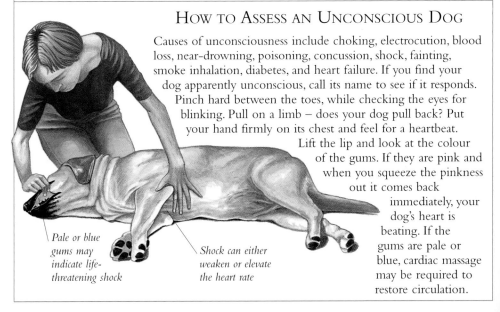

Pale or blue gums may indicate life-threatening shock

Shock can either weaken or elevate the heart rate

ARTIFICIAL RESPIRATION AND CARDIAC MASSAGE

Do not attempt to give artificial respiration or heart massage unless your dog is unconscious and will die without your help. If your dog has been pulled from water, suspend it by its hind legs for at least 30 seconds to drain the air passages. If it has been electrocuted, do not touch it until the electricity is turned off. If it has choked, press forcefully over the ribs to dislodge the object. Never put yourself at risk; if possible share first-aid procedures with someone else or have them telephone the nearest veterinarian and arrange transport.

Tongue is pulled forwards and debris removed

Hold muzzle shut and seal your mouth over dog's nostrils

1 Place your dog on its side, ideally with its head slightly lower than the rest of its body – elevation of the hindquarters sends more blood to the brain. Clear the airway by straightening the neck, pulling the tongue fully forwards, and sweeping the mouth with two fingers to remove any excess saliva or obstructions. Also ensure that the nose is not clogged with mucus or debris. If you cannot hear the heart, start cardiac massage at once.

2 Close the mouth, hold the muzzle with both hands, and place your mouth around the nose. Blow in until you see the chest expand, then let the lungs naturally deflate. Repeat this 10–20 times per minute, checking the pulse every 10 seconds to make sure the heart is beating.

Pumping forces blood towards brain

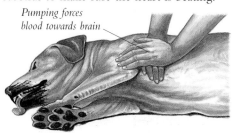

3 If the heart has stopped, begin cardiac massage immediately. Place the heel of one hand on the left side of the chest just behind the elbow, then the heel of your other hand on top. Press vigorously down and forwards, pumping 80–100 times per minute. Alternate 20–25 cardiac massages with 10 seconds of mouth-to-nose respiration until the heart beats, restoring colour to the gums. Continue resuscitation until breathing starts. A very fat Labrador should be laid on its back and pressed on the chest for cardiac massage.

ALWAYS LOOK FOR SHOCK

Shock is a potentially life-endangering condition which occurs when the body's circulation fails. It can be caused by vomiting, diarrhoea, poisons, animal bites, a twisted stomach, bleeding, and many other illnesses or accidents, and onset may not be apparent for several hours. The signs include pale or blue gums, rapid breathing, a faint or quickened pulse, cold extremities, and general weakness. Treating shock takes precedence over other injuries, including fractures. Your priorities are to control any bleeding, maintain body heat, and support vital functions. Unless shock is the result of heatstroke, wrap your dog loosely in a warm blanket, elevate its hindquarters, stabilize breathing and the heart if necessary using mouth-to-nose resuscitation and cardiac massage, and seek urgent medical advice.

MINOR INJURY AND ILLNESS

EVERY OWNER SHOULD KNOW how to administer medicines and other basic treatment to their dog in the event of accident or illness. Injuries to ears and paws, from fights or sharp objects, are not uncommon, and may require prompt bandaging and precautionary restraint before a vet is called.

APPLYING AN EMERGENCY BANDAGE TO THE EAR

Assistant kneels behind, keeping injured dog still

Reassure your dog while giving first aid

1 While an assistant soothes and steadies your dog, apply clean, preferably non-stick, absorbent material to the wound. Take care you are not bitten through fright. Cut a section from a pair of tights and slip it over your hands.

2 With your assistant holding the absorbent pad in place, slip the tights over your dog's head. This will hold the ear firmly, helping the blood to clot. Ensure that the windpipe receives no undue pressure.

BANDAGING A WOUNDED PAW

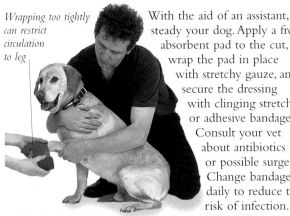

Wrapping too tightly can restrict circulation to leg

With the aid of an assistant, steady your dog. Apply a fresh, absorbent pad to the cut, wrap the pad in place with stretchy gauze, and secure the dressing with clinging stretch or adhesive bandage. Consult your vet about antibiotics or possible surgery. Change bandages daily to reduce the risk of infection.

Bandage allows air into wound

3 If necessary, secure the tights at each end with tape to prevent your dog from removing the bandage with its paws. However, this is only a temporary cover, and your veterinarian should examine the injury.

IMPROVISING A MUZZLE

Always apply a muzzle for safety unless breathing is impaired

1 Even the most loving animal is capable of accidentally biting when hurt. With an assistant holding your dog still, make a loop with any soft material such as tights, gauze, or a tie, and slip it over the muzzle.

2 With the loop in place, tighten it gently. Then bring both lengths of material down and cross them under the jaws. If your dog is confused or upset, speak to it in a relaxed, comforting tone as you proceed.

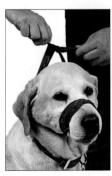

3 To complete the process, wrap the material round the back of the ears and tie the ends securely in a knot. With the emergency muzzle fastened, you can then safely give attention to specific injuries elsewhere.

ADMINISTERING MEDICINES

Tablet can be hidden in favourite food

GIVING A PILL
With your dog seated, open its mouth and insert the pill as far back as possible. Then hold the jaw shut and tilt it upwards, stroking the neck to induce swallowing.

Cough syrup is taken easily from syringe

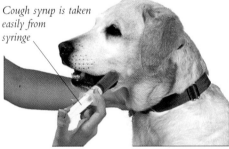

GIVING LIQUIDS
Using a syringe from your vet or a chemist, squirt the medicine into the mouth, not down the throat where it may enter the windpipe. Hold your dog's muzzle until it swallows.

USING AN ELIZABETHAN COLLAR

Your vet may provide a lampshade-shaped collar for your convalescent dog, to prevent any scratching or chewing at wounds. This collar should be left on whenever your dog is alone, but may be removed at mealtimes or during exercise on a lead, when you can deter self-inflicted damage. The device is cumbersome and likely to be worn with resignation!

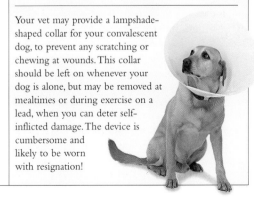

ORIGINS OF THE BREED

THE LABRADOR'S PROBABLE source is the Lesser Newfoundland or St. John's Dog, perhaps intermingled with dogs brought to Canada's shores by European fishermen. Today's Labrador was refined through English breeding, while the original dogs from Newfoundland are the basis for many other breeds.

HISTORY OF THE LABRADOR RETRIEVER

CANADIAN ANCESTORS

By the early 1800s there were two distinct types of dog in Newfoundland – large, heavy-coated dogs used as draught animals and for collecting nets, and smaller, dense-coated dogs worked as retrievers on land and water. Admired for their skills and loyalty, they were brought to England by local fishermen until 1885, when Newfoundland destroyed its dogs to promote sheep farming.

ORIGINAL NEWFOUNDLAND

FIRST LABRADOR BREEDERS

The dog's hardy constitution and fine retrieving abilities were noted by English landowners, who purchased them for gun work. Aristocrats, notably the Earls of Malmesbury and Dukes of Buccleuch, developed successful breeding programmes and created intense interest in the new "Labrador" as a sporting dog. Colonel Peter Hawker and Lord Knutsford were also instrumental in establishing the breed and its official standard.

6TH DUKE OF BUCCLEUCH

NEAREST RELATIVES

NEWFOUNDLAND
Derived from Greater Newfoundland or St. John's Dog

Although now quite different in size, the Newfoundland and Labrador probably have similar origins in mastiffs and working dogs taken to Canada by Portuguese, Basque, and English fishermen. Today, they share the same equable disposition, and are both physically and temperamentally not too distant from Iberian breeds such as the Portuguese Cattle Dog. The original dogs from Newfoundland are the root stock of all retrievers. Chesapeake Bay Retrievers descend from dogs taken directly to Maryland. Curly-coated and Flat-coated Retrievers are the result of cross-breeding with regional English dogs, while Golden Retrievers – so resembling Labradors in character and utility – are, in fact, more distant descendants, derived from Flat-coats.

CURLY-COATED RETRIEVER
*Early Labradors crossed with now-extinct
English Water Spaniel*

THE CURIOUS LABRADOODLE

The Labrador's co-operative nature makes it an ideal service dog – easy to train, and an affable companion for the disabled. However, its hair is shed heavily, creating problems for people allergic to dog dander. Therefore, in an attempt to develop a non-moulting dog with the Labrador's responsive and easy-going character, Australian breeders in 1989 began crossing Labradors with Standard Poodles. The resulting Labradoodle is certainly distinctive, but while the combination appears to produce a genial temperament, the non-shedding characteristic has not yet become a fixed attribute.

FLAT-COATED RETRIEVER
*Produced by crossing Greater
and Lesser St. John's Dogs, then
crossing the result with Setters*

GOLDEN RETRIEVER
*Flat-coated Retriever crossed with
now-extinct Tweed Water Spaniel*

CHESAPEAKE BAY RETRIEVER
*Result of Lesser St. John's Dogs
bred with local American hounds*

PORTUGUESE CATTLE DOG
*Working breed used by Basque
and Portuguese fishermen may
be distant ancestor of Labrador*

REPRODUCTION

PRODUCING A LITTER of Labrador Retriever puppies is in itself easy, since both male and female Labradors are naturally good breeders. However, the decision to mate your dog must be made responsibly – following sound professional guidance, and always with the best interest of the breed at heart.

THE MATING INSTINCT

Healthy males as young as 10 months can be used for mating. It is best to wait until a female is about two years old, in roughly her third oestrous cycle, when she is emotionally prepared for a litter. Ovulation usually occurs 10-12 days after the first sign of bleeding and vulvar swelling. The most successful matings generally take place on the male's home turf.

PREGNANCY DIAGNOSIS

Ovulation, the optimum time to mate, is accurately indicated by an increased level of the hormone progesterone in the blood. Pregnancy, however, cannot be confirmed by blood or urine tests. An ultrasound scan at three weeks or a physical examination slightly later remain the best means of diagnosis.

Ultrasound scan shows several puppies in womb

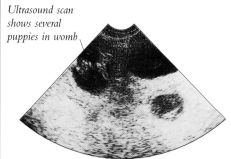

DEALING WITH MISMATING

Mismatings can be avoided by keeping a watchful eye on your bitch when in season, by using tablets or injections to prevent ovulation, or by spaying. If an unwanted mating does occur, contact your vet. A pregnancy can be terminated, usually within three days of mating, with a hormone injection. This will induce an immediate repeat season, demanding renewed vigilance for 8–15 days after the beginning of vaginal discharge.

SPECIAL NEEDS OF AN EXPECTANT BITCH

During the first month of pregnancy, a bitch should continue to exercise freely. Thereafter, the increasing weight of the litter will naturally make her slower and less agile. At this stage, swimming is good exercise, but avoid very cold water. After the sixth week, food intake should be gradually increased so that by the time her puppies are due, a bitch will be consuming 30 per cent more than her normal daily quantity. Ensure that the diet provides an adequate but not excessive amount of calcium.

MALE AND FEMALE REPRODUCTIVE SYSTEMS

A bitch comes into season twice yearly, is fertile for three days during each cycle, and will be receptive to mating only during these periods. Males, however, willingly mate year round. For the female, ovulation continues throughout life and there is no menopause, although breeding in later years is risky. Pregnancy lasts for about 63 days.

RESPONSIBLE BREEDING

If planning to breed from your Labrador, seek professional advice from your vet or from an experienced and reputable breeder. Ensure that the prospective parents' physical and emotional attributes will enhance the breed. Both partners should be screened for certain inherited diseases such as progressive retinal atrophy and hip dysplasia, via an eye examination and a hip X-ray. Your vet may also advise testing for brucellosis, a canine venereal disease. Remember that Labrador litters are large, usually about eight puppies, and that you will be responsible for finding each offspring a safe home.

PREVENTING PREGNANCY

Neutering is the most effective and safest means of preventing pregnancy. The female, because she carries the young, is the usual candidate. Both the ovaries and the uterus are removed, followed by a week's rest. The procedure for males involves simple surgery on the scrotum for removal of the testicles.

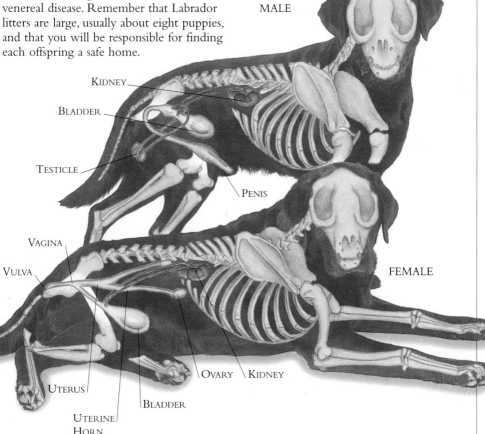

MALE

KIDNEY

BLADDER

TESTICLE

PENIS

VAGINA

VULVA

FEMALE

OVARY   KIDNEY

UTERUS

BLADDER

UTERINE
HORN

PRE- AND POST-WHELPING

AS THE DAY OF BIRTH approaches, introduce the expectant mother to her whelping box and arrange for your vet to be on call in case of problems. Although Labradors seldom have difficulties, it is best to have experienced help both at the delivery and later, for after-care of weak puppies.

INTRODUCING A WHELPING BOX

Several weeks before she is due to deliver, familiarize the mother-to-be with her whelping box. The box should have a length and width of at least 1.2 m (4 ft), and be made of marine ply, which will not be damaged by birth fluids. Three sides should be 45–50 cm (18–20 in) high to prevent the puppies from wandering off, while the fourth should have a lockable opening to allow the mother easy access. Start collecting newspaper; you will need several bundles to line the box and to serve as bedding for the new puppies for the next two months.

Expectant mother feels secure in her purpose-made whelping "den"

DELIVERY CARE

If you have never been present at a birth, ask an experienced dog breeder to attend, and inform your vet when labour begins. Keep the room temperature at around 25° C (77° F). If after two hours your bitch does not produce a puppy, contact your vet once again for advice. The puppy's position may need manipulating to facilitate delivery. Although uncommon, some Labradors do require a Caesarean section. Place a warm, towel-covered hot-water bottle in a cardboard box, and keep this nearby as a safe receptacle for each newly-delivered puppy. The box may also be used to transport the puppies if mother and litter need to be taken to the vet.

SIGNS OF IMPENDING BIRTH

Your bitch is likely to refuse food shortly before she goes into labour. She will restlessly seek out her whelping box and start to tear up the bedding, preparing a nest for her puppies. Her body temperature will drop, and she may pant. When her waters break and contractions begin, birth is imminent. Keep other animals and strangers away during the labour.

THE NEW LITTER

Towel-dry each puppy after it is delivered, and clear its nose of mucus; all newborns should squeal and wriggle. During whelping, offer the mother drinks of warm milk. Let her rest after labour has ended and all placentas have been delivered. Place each puppy by a teat to suckle. The mother will also require plenty of nourishment in the coming weeks – at peak lactation, up to four times her normal intake.

ASSISTING A WEAK OR ABANDONED PUPPY

HELPING TO SUCKLE

On average, one out of seven puppies is born relatively small and weak. Runts are often the least healthy of the litter, and if left to nature frequently die within a few days. To aid survival, place a frail puppy near the teats offering the best supply of milk.

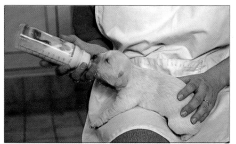

BOTTLE FEEDING

In large, healthy litters where there simply is not enough milk to feed all the puppies, or when the mother is incapacitated or abandons her offspring, use canine milk formula as a supplement. Bottle feed initially every two to three hours, seeking your vet's guidance on the correct quantities.

GROWING TOGETHER

After three weeks, the puppies begin to explore; by 12 weeks, their senses are fully developed. Handle and groom all puppies often, so they learn to accept being touched by humans, but do not upset the protective mother. Gentle exposure to new sights and sounds now will help the puppies to grow into well-adjusted, adaptable adults.

Puppies huddle together for security

PREPARING FOR A SHOW

TAKING PART IN a dog show can be great fun, but both you and your Labrador should be fully prepared. Teach your dog show manners, and make sure it is in prime condition, as it will be judged against a breed standard of ideal physical and personality characteristics typifying the "perfect" specimen.

BASIC EQUIPMENT FOR YOU AND YOUR DOG

FOR HANDLING AND SECURITY

You will need a non-check show collar that permits the judge to have an unimpeded view of your dog's neck, and a slim lead about 1.5 m (5 ft) long. If attending a "benched" event, take a benching chain to secure your dog in its allotted space, as well as an identification number clip.

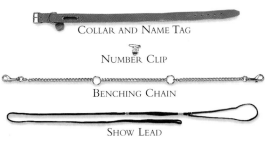

COLLAR AND NAME TAG

NUMBER CLIP

BENCHING CHAIN

SHOW LEAD

TRANSPORT AND SUPPLIES

Your dog will travel best in a crate loaded in the back of a car. Pack food and water for your dog, along with its bowls. If you plan to picnic, also take refreshments for yourself. Folding chairs and a large umbrella for sun or rain protection are essential, as are plastic bags or a "poop scoop" to clear up your dog's mess. A towel is useful for cleaning muddy paws. All supplies, including grooming equipment, should be kept in a designated bag.

MEETING SHOW STANDARDS

Visit shows alone first to see exactly what occurs. While working trials require dogs well-trained in obedience and a variety of specialized skills, kennel club events demand only beauty and personality. For these, your dog's coat must be in good condition, its ears clear of wax, and the teeth tartar-free. Bathe your dog and clip its nails a few days before a show, to allow renewal of the coat's gloss by natural oils. Use a coat conditioner only with the advice of experienced exhibitors. Remember, no cosmetic aids to improve a dog's looks are permitted at shows.

Owner checks dog's appearance before entering show ring

TRAINING AND TEMPERAMENT FOR THE RING

ACCEPTING CLOSE EXAMINATION

A successful show dog has been trained from puppyhood to accept scrutiny from strangers. Reward your dog for permitting unfamiliar people to handle it as a ring judge would – allowing the hindquarters to be touched, and the mouth to be opened and the teeth examined. Judges prefer dogs that are amenable as well as handsome.

LEARNING TO STAND FOR INSPECTION

Young Labradors in particular often wiggle with excitement when touched. Create a show-ring environment at home, where your dog can learn to stand still while being inspected. Train with food treats – acceptable bribes in real shows. With maturity, most Labradors become calmer in the ring.

STAYING LIVELY AND ALERT

A dog show is exciting for owners because of the hope of winning, and exciting for canines since it is an opportunity to meet many other dogs. However, by the time your dog is due to enter the ring, it may be bored, and bored dogs do not win prizes. Labradors revive instantly at the scent of food. Use favourite treats to keep your dog bright and animated while performing for the show judge.

Dog is rewarded with food treat for standing in show position, tail out and head high

COSTS OF SHOWING

Showing your Labrador Retriever can be inexpensive, or surprisingly costly. If you show your own dog, your only expenses are entry fees, transport, and accommodation. At the highest levels on the show circuit, professional trainers and handlers are frequently employed. This can add a very considerable financial burden, and it is a rare dog that is so successful that handling costs are earned back in stud fees or puppy prices. If you are not interested in serious exhibiting, a more sensible approach to showing your Labrador is to consider it a pleasurable pastime for both you and your dog.

WHAT HAPPENS AT A SHOW

EXHIBITING EVENTS RANGE from informal local competitions, to open shows for all breeds, to exclusive Labrador championships. Each has its own rules, but all follow similar principles in the quest to find a truly outstanding dog. Shows can provide a very sociable and rewarding day out for owners and canines alike.

SETTLING IN AT THE BENCHES

At most shows, dogs remain with their owners, but at some events your Labrador will be housed at a numbered "bench". Secure your dog with a benching chain and offer it a drink of water. Have someone sit by the bench so your dog does not become bored or lonely, and postpone meals until after it is shown to keep it active and alert.

ADJUSTING THE "STAND"

For show presentation, your dog must adopt an appropriate stance. Train it from an early age to stand on command with its tail out, legs straight, and head held high. During the judge's examination, you should interfere as little as possible, but you may encourage correct posture by using eye contact. Be cautious with food rewards; they can be over-exciting or may cause your dog to salivate unattractively.

With subtle knee gesture, owner coaches dog to lift head

JUDGE'S INSPECTION

When called, enter the ring and set your Labrador in its "show stance". The judge will examine the body in detail to see how closely it conforms to the breed standard. Your dog's temperament is being noted too, and any nervousness, resistance, or aggression will be viewed unfavourably.

LINE-UP OF FINALISTS

After the individual assessments, a short list of five or six dogs is chosen and re-inspected. The judge will then place the finalists in order of merit, awarding rosettes for first, second, and third place, as well as for "reserve" and "highly commended" contenders.

ASSESSMENT OF THE GAIT

The judge will ask for each dog to be walked round the ring, to appraise its movement. Dogs should "gait" with confidence and fluid grace; a stilted or hesitant manner will be penalized. Symmetry between dog and handler is also important. Some Labradors are natural show-offs and relish parading in the ring.

EXCITEMENT OF PARTICIPATING

At the highest levels of exhibiting, training and ring handling are performed by professionals. In lesser leagues, owners show their own dogs, and attend events as an enjoyable hobby, offering friendly competition and the chance to socialize with like-minded people – all in all, a pleasant day's outing.

BEST OF BREED

Winning dogs will have the physical attributes of a champion along with a "star" personality. It is a tremendous achievement if your Labrador has captured a prize. Yet ideal looks and show style are not the sole criteria of an outstanding dog; any dog in glowing health and with a fine temperament is just as much a winner. Countless "champions" are never seen in a show ring.

SPECIALIZED TRAINING

LABRADORS THRIVE ON THE challenge of advanced training, and their responsive nature and eagerness to please make them adept competitors in obedience, agility, and field trials. The Labrador's keen scenting abilities, "soft mouth", and strong retrieval instinct also give it superb potential as a gundog.

FIELD AND HUNTING ROLES

RETRIEVE TRAINING

Sand-filled dummy is returned carefully to owner's hand

Before practising retrieves, a dog must be well controlled, reliably walking to heel and always coming when called. After your Labrador has learned to hold and then give a canvas-covered dummy gently to hand, teach it to wait while the dummy is thrown before fetching it on command. Attend gundog classes to master relevant whistle, verbal, and directional commands, and retrieves from all types of cover as well as in and across water. Formal training accustoms your dog to working on unfamiliar terrain and with the distraction of other dogs and handlers.

SELECTING THE RIGHT PUPPY FOR TRAINING

All Labradors share an instinctive desire to retrieve, and have been bred to respond well to human direction. They are also "soft mouthed" – able to hold items gently. With dedicated tuition, most Labradors can be trained in advanced obedience, agility, or gunwork. However, various kennels specialize in producing dogs for different roles, especially field trials and the show ring. Field trialling requires nimbleness, swift response to command, and highly developed scenting skills. If you plan to enter this very competitive sport, seek advice from a successful field-trial trainer on selecting the most suitable puppy.

WORKING TO THE GUN

With the supervision of an experienced trainer, introduce your dog to gunfire, then work on scenting and tenderly collecting freshly-killed game. In field trials and at hunts, dogs must be steady at all times, never chasing unshot game, and only leaving your side when instructed.

ADVANCED OBEDIENCE TRIALS

SUSTAINED LIE-DOWN ON COMMAND
Competitive obedience trials provide excellent mental stimulation. Begin classes at six months, after your dog has mastered walking on a lead and basic commands. Advanced training includes close and fast-pace heelwork, retrieves, recalls, distant control, sustained sit/downs (sometimes for as long as 10 minutes with the handler out of sight), send-away/down/return sequences, and scent discrimination.

RETRIEVING A DUMB-BELL
Labradors have a natural advantage in retrieval tests, and can be trained to high levels. Beginning with a dumb-bell, dogs progress to fetching items provided by the trials judge.

TRAINING IN AGILITY

NEGOTIATING OBSTACLES
Agility courses open to all dogs are run against time. The Labrador is not as fast as some other breeds, but can be very nimble if enthusiasm is restrained. To be successful, your dog must respond well off a lead and tackle obstacles only on your command.

TIPPING A SEE-SAW
Agility work requires dexterity, confidence, and instant response to command, and can be a productive channel for restless energy. Standard trial apparatus includes an "A" frame, hurdles, a tyre, poles to weave through, a tunnel, and a see-saw. Training demands ample patience; start when your dog is a year old by enrolling in a local club. Make sure that both you and your Labrador are sufficiently fit to participate.

ASSISTANCE ROLES

THE LABRADOR HAS a variety of inbred attributes which make it an ideal service dog. Its genial nature, responsiveness to training, and retrieving abilities are invaluable in assisting the disabled, while its gundog's nose has been well employed in scent trailing for search and rescue or detection roles.

BRED AND TRAINED AS A HELPING COMPANION

EARLY TRAINING

Labrador Retrievers and Labrador cross-breeds are the most popular dogs for assisting the blind. The largest guide-dog training centres breed their own stock. Puppies live in volunteers' homes, where they receive basic training and are exposed to a range of learning scenarios.

MAKING OF A GUIDE DOG

The Labrador's medium size, eagerness to please, receptiveness to training, and, above all, its steady temperament make it ideal for assistance work. In breeding programmes, dogs are selectively bred for a calm, sensible attitude in unusual situations, ensuring a low drop-out rate – less than 30 per cent – during the subsequent months of formal training at regional guide-dog centres.

EYES FOR THE BLIND

Since guide dogs and owners typically share their lives for eight to nine years, it is important that their personalities are compatible. Training-centre staff initially assess the relationship during a period of residential instruction, where both dog and prospective owner learn to understand each other. After the pair have "graduated", specialized staff make home visits to ensure that the partnership is working well.

HOME HELP

As natural retrievers, Labradors enjoy carrying objects and can easily be trained to fetch common household items, to help the infirm or disabled. Dogs with particularly gregarious characters can act as ears for deaf people, alerting their owners to important sounds, such as a doorbell ringing or a baby crying. Sometimes, young guide dogs that prove too active for the role are retrained as "hearing" dogs.

CROSS-BRED FOR IMPROVED HEALTH

Because its personality is similar to the Labrador, the Golden Retriever is also used in a vast range of service capacities, as a guide dog for the blind and in other specialized assistance roles. To reduce the risk of breed-related genetic disorders, ranging from arthritis to blindness, the two breeds are often crossed, producing puppies that are both temperamentally sound and less prone to inherited ailments.

MOBILITY FOR THE DISABLED

A Labrador can be taught to meet the specific needs of its disabled owner – to pull a wheelchair along, pick up dropped items, open certain types of door, stand and push lift buttons, or even to open clothes dryers and take out the washing! All these activities provide physical and mental stimulation for the well-trained dog. An added bonus is that a disabled person will often be acknowledged and approached much more readily when accompanied by a friendly canine assistant.

SCENT-TRAILING SKILLS FOR SEARCH AND RESCUE

In earthquakes and avalanches, search and rescue Labradors trained to follow air and ground scent trails perform well. Many also help to locate people lost in mountainous regions. The first cave-probing search and rescue dog was a Labrador, who successfully navigated a labyrinth of subterranean passageways to lead a stranded party to safety. The breed's scent-detecting roles have extended to work with police forces, tracking illicit drugs. Labradors have also been employed in Scandinavia to uncover mould in timber yards, and in the United Kingdom to reveal rising damp in homes.

BREED STANDARD

A BREED STANDARD is used by the governing kennel club of each country to describe the ideal Labrador Retriever. Show dogs are judged against this formal index of the unique physical qualities, demeanour, and personality traits that characterize a "perfect" specimen of the breed.

LABRADOR RETRIEVER
GUNDOG GROUP
(Last revised March 1994)

Reproduced by kind permission of
The Kennel Club
London, England

GENERAL APPEARANCE
Strongly built, short-coupled, very active; broad in skull; broad and deep through chest and ribs; broad and strong over loins and hindquarters.

CHARACTERISTICS
Good-tempered, very agile. Excellent nose, soft mouth; keen love of water. Adaptable, devoted companion.

TEMPERAMENT
Intelligent, keen and biddable, with a strong will to please. Kindly nature, with no trace of aggression or undue shyness.

HEAD AND SKULL
Skull broad with defined stop; clean-cut without fleshy cheeks. Jaws of medium length, powerful not snipy. Nose wide, nostrils well developed.

EYES
Medium size, expressing intelligence and good temper; brown or hazel.

EARS
Not large or heavy, hanging close to head and set rather far back.

MOUTH
Jaws and teeth strong with a perfect, regular and complete scissor bite, i.e. upper teeth closely overlapping lower teeth and set square to the jaws.

NECK
Clean, strong, powerful, set into well placed shoulders.

FOREQUARTERS
Shoulders long and sloping. Forelegs well boned and straight from elbow to ground when viewed from either front or side.

BODY
Chest of good width and depth, with well sprung barrel ribs. Level topline. Loins wide, short-coupled and strong.

HINDQUARTERS
Well developed, not sloping to tail; well turned stifle. Hocks well let down, cowhocks highly undesirable.

FEET
Round, compact; well arched toes and well developed pads.

TAIL
Distinctive feature, very thick towards base, gradually tapering towards tip, medium length, free from feathering, but clothed thickly all round with short, thick, dense coat, thus giving "rounded" appearance described as "Otter" tail. May be carried gaily but should not curl over back.

GAIT/MOVEMENT
Free, covering adequate ground; straight and true in front and rear.

COAT
Distinctive feature, short dense without wave or feathering, giving fairly hard feel to the touch; weather-resistant undercoat.

COLOUR

Wholly black, yellow or liver/chocolate. Yellows range from light cream to red fox. Small white spot on chest permissible.

SIZE

Ideal height at withers:
dogs: 56–57 cms (22–22½ ins);
bitches: 54–56 cms (21½–22 ins).

FAULTS

Any departure from the foregoing points should be considered a fault and the seriousness with which the fault should be regarded should be in exact proportion to its degree.

NOTE

Male animals should have two apparently normal testicles fully descended into the scrotum.

GLOSSARY

BARREL Rounded rib section.

COW-HOCKED When the hocks turn inwards towards each other.

ELBOW The joint between the upper arm and the forearm.

FEATHERING Longer fringe of hair on ears, legs, tail or body.

FOREARM The bone of the forelegs between elbow and wrist.

FORELEG The front leg from elbow to foot.

FOREQUARTERS Front part of dog excluding head and neck.

GAIT The pattern of footsteps at various rates of speed, each pattern distinguished by a particular rhythm and footfall.

GAY TAIL The tail carried very high or over dog's back. A term sometimes used when a tail is carried higher than the carriage approved in the breed standard.

GUN DOG A dog trained to work to find live game and/or retrieve game that has been shot or wounded.

HIND LEG Leg from pelvis to foot.

HINDQUARTERS Rear part of dog from loin.

HOCK The tarsus or collection of bones of the hind leg forming the joint between the second thigh and the metatarsus.

LIVER A colour, also known as brown or chocolate.

LOIN Region of the body on either side of vertebral column between the last ribs and the hindquarters.

METATARSALS Bones between the hock joint and foot.

MUZZLE The head in front of the eyes, nasal bone, nostrils, and jaws; foreface.

OCCIPUT Upper, back point of skull.

OTTER TAIL Thick at the root, tapering to blunt end with short thick hair growing round tail, not extending below hock.

SHORT-COUPLED With very short coupling [The part of the body between the ribs and pelvis; the loin].

SKULL Bony regions of head. Usually meant as section of head from stop to occiput.

SNIPY A pointed, weak muzzle.

SOFT MOUTH Gentle grip on a retrieve.

STIFLE The joint of the hind leg between the thigh and the second thigh; the dog's knee.

STOP The step up from muzzle to skull; indentation between the eyes where the nasal bone and skull meet.

TOPLINE The dog's outline from just behind the withers to the tail set.

UNDERCOAT Dense, soft, short coat concealed by longer top-coat.

WELL SPRUNG RIBS Ribs springing out from spinal column giving correct shape.

WITHERS The highest point of the body, immediately behind the neck.

INDEX

ACKNOWLEDGMENTS

AUTHOR'S ACKNOWLEDGMENTS

Many thanks to all those who were involved in the production of this handbook, with particular gratitude to Patricia Holden White for choreographing several photographic sessions, Gary Clayton Jones for supplying X-rays, Peter Kertesz for lending photographs of teeth, and Ivan Gerger at the Waltham Centre of Pet Nutrition for providing advice on the Labrador's energy requirements.

PUBLISHER'S ACKNOWLEDGMENTS

Dorling Kindersley would like to thank photographer Tracy Morgan for her invaluable contribution to the book. Also special thanks to Tracy's photographic assistants: Sally Bergh-Roose, Stella Smyth-Carpenter, and Christina Hale. We are also very grateful to Patricia Holden White for her generous advice and help on photographic sessions. Thanks also to Karin Woodruff for the index, and to Sarah Kendall of The Company of Animals for supplying props. A very special thank you to the staff of the Breeding Centre, Guide Dogs for the Blind Association, Tollgate House, Warwickshire, especially to Neil Ewart, Helen Freeman, and Alison Morton, whose expert guidance, tireless assistance, and endless supply of puppies were crucial in completing several sections of the book. Finally, we would like to thank the following people for lending their dogs and/or for modelling:

Kane and Mitchell Andrews; Sally Bergh-Roose; Ken, Chris, and Sheryl Brooks (Pepsi); Penny Carpanini (SHCH Covetwood Elouise of Carpenny "Soda" and Tabathas Mirth "Mirth"); Suzanne Collins (Karma); Gail Cornish (Romy); Mr. and Mrs. J. Denton (Icarus Kentucky Rain); Mr. and Mrs. Egan and Yvonne Egan (Noble Adventurer "Jack"); Claire Folkard; Bruce Fogle; Jill Fornary; Homer Gilpin; Donald Goddard (Billy), Sarah and Victoria Goodwin; Christina Hale; Sally Lewis (the Gamesmere Gundogs: Wendy, Pippa, Anna, and Storm); Sarah Lillicrapp; John and Alison Lloyd (Tara); Tracy Morgan (Craigleith Music Man "Topper"); Adrian and Glen Mustoe (Henry and Minnie); Seán O'Connell; Rosalind Ormiston (Sammy and Chip); Marilyn Prior (SHCH Perfick Gent of Priorise "Biggles", Landacre Cute Sophie of Priorise "Sophie", and Daisy); Susan Proctor (Kegeth); Jacky Rappaport (Oscar); Jane Russell; Hester Small; Stella and Stephanie Smyth-Carpenter (Dinah); Sue Webb (Tara).

PHOTOGRAPHIC CREDITS

Key: l=left, r=right, t=top, c=centre, a=above, b=below

All photography by Tracy Morgan except:
Animal Photography: (Sally Anne Thompson) 6bl, 15bl, 56cl, 72br, 74bl; **Christopher Bradbury:** 19a, 64cl, 64cr, 67cl, 67t, 67cr; **John Darling:** 2, 7bl, 7r, 42, 72cl; **Dogs for the Disabled:** 75tl; **Mary Evans Picture Library:** 6cr, 62cl; **Guide Dogs for the Blind Association:** 74br; **The Hulton Deutsch Collection:** 62cr; **The Image Bank:** (Lynn M. Stone) 6tl; **Impact Photos:** (Alex MacNaughton) 73bl, (Sally Fear) 74c; **Dave King:** 22bl, 62b; **Rex Features:** (Sipa Press) 75c, 75b; **Tim Ridley:** 8br, 14cl, 17cl, 28–29, 30–31, 37b, 37tl, 37tr, 41b, 42–43, 44br, 44cl, 44cr, 45br, 50b, 50t, 51b, 60bl, 60br, 60cl, 60cr, 61br, 68cr, 70t; **Science Photo Library:** David Scharf 52bl; **David Ward:** 18cl, 26b, 41c.

ILLUSTRATIONS

Samantha Elmhurst: 52–53, 55, 65;
Sean Milne: 58–59;
Jane Pickering: 35;
Clive Spong: 11.